The Return of the King

An Overview of the New Testament: Part Four

Bob Evely

To Jill

The wife of my youth.
My best friend.
Most definitely my better half.
An amazing wife, mother, and grandma.

You have made this spiritual journey with me,
Every step of the way.

You have always supported me in all that I do.

I appreciate you far more
than words could possibly express.

With love,

Bob

"Return of the King"
Abby Evely

"Return of the King"
Livy Evely (abstract artist)

An Overview of the New Testament

New Testament: Part Four

𝕿𝖍𝖊 𝕽𝖊𝖙𝖚𝖗𝖓 𝖔𝖋 𝖙𝖍𝖊 𝕶𝖎𝖓𝖌

The Unveiling of Jesus Christ

The last book of the Bible,

Commonly referred to as

"Revelation"

"The Unveiling of Jesus Christ, which God gives to Him,
to show His slaves what must occur swiftly."(1:1)

𝕭𝖔𝖇 𝕰𝖛𝖊𝖑𝖞.

*Scriptures taken from the Concordant Literal New Testament
and the Concordant Version of the Old Testament unless otherwise noted.
Concordant Publishing Concern, 15570 West Knochaven Road,
Santa Clarita, CA 91387 (www.Concordant.org)*

𝕲𝖗𝖆𝖈𝖊 𝕰𝖛𝖆𝖓𝖌𝖊𝖑 𝕱𝖊𝖑𝖑𝖔𝖜𝖘𝖍𝖎𝖕:

P O Box 6, Wilmore, KY 40390

www.GraceEvangel.org

The Return of the King; An Overview of the New Testament – Part Four
by Bob Evely
Copyright © 2018 by Robert W. Evely

First Printing: 2018

ISBN 978-1-7323228-9-9

Cover created by Cris Evely
Front: Evely family & friends (drone photo by Kari Cheek)
Back: Drawing by Elinor Evely

Published by:
Robert W. Evely
P.O. Box 6
Wilmore, KY 40390

www.GraceEvangel.org

Table of Contents

Return of the King
Preliminary Thoughts

An Overview of the Scriptures, by
BOB EVELY © 2018.
An Independent Minister of Christ Jesus
Of the church at Wilmore, Kentucky

J. Vernon McGee once noted that if he was teaching on the Book of Revelation he could fill the church, even during midweek services. But if he taught on Romans he could empty the church. "There are people who will run all the way across this area to find out from a speaker just how many hairs are in the horse's tail in Revelation." McGee reported that he was once told by Dr. Arno Gaebelein, "There are a great many people more interested in Antichrist than they are in Christ."

As we prepare to consider Revelation let us cast aside all interpretations that have influenced us to this point, and let us read the book afresh. E. W. Bullinger aptly states: "The mists of tradition have been allowed to take the place of independent research. Tradition is like the tether which prevents an animal from getting a blade of grass beyond the length of that tether." Much of theology found in orthodoxy, creeds, and popular Christian teaching is based upon *tradition*, not God's Word, and suffers from a "tethering" which prevents the seeker of truth from finding it.

If we rely upon traditional Bible translations and the popular teachings of today's church relative to our study of Revelation, we will have been tethered to those teachings and unable to observe any truths that may have eluded the church. A careful, consistent translation of the Bible from its original languages will clearly reveal that much truth has been confused and clouded, and much of what God has revealed is lost to those depending upon modern, inconsistent Bible translations and the shallow, tethered teachings of today's church leaders.

We must consider the precise words employed by God in His revelation to mankind. Only then will we see distinctions that God is making in His revelation. And only then will the truth become known to us.

Unfortunately, today's church is not so careful as to do this. Again turning to Bullinger: "No matter what part of the Bible may be read, the one object seems to be to find the Church. For, the Word of truth not being rightly divided, or indeed divided at all, the whole Bible is

5

supposed to be about every one, in every part, and in every age; and the Church is supposed to be its one pervading subject."

By carelessly, or at times purposefully, combining all things revealed in Scripture without observing to whom or in what age a word pertains makes it *impossible* to discern what God is revealing to us. God may be revealing a certain truth that pertained to *Israel*, and perhaps only for a particular period of time. Yet the church today will often substitute *the church* for Israel, claiming something for ourselves that does not pertain to us at all. Thus, that which God has revealed to us is lost or distorted.

If care is taken in our handling of the truths found in Revelation, we will see that **it does not pertain to the church** (the Body of Christ) at all. Its subject is God's dealings with ISRAEL, and with the Gentile nations, in a time AFTER the Body of Christ has been removed from the earth.

The Body of Christ is not to be found anywhere in the book of Revelation!

Thus there is need for a careful, consistent translation of the Scriptures, as most popular Bible translations of our day have contributed to the confusion by incorporating opinion and interpretation into God's Word. Once again we hear from Mr. Bullinger: "Let us say at once that we believe, and must believe (1), that God means what He says; and (2), that He has a meaning for every word that He says. All His works and all His words are perfect, in their choice, order and place: so perfect, that, if one word or expression is used, there is a reason why no other would have done."

Of the book of Revelation, Bullinger notes: "It is not only Hebrew in character as to its linguistic peculiarities, but especially in its use of the Old Testament. ... All who know anything of Old Testament history cannot fail to detect the almost constant reference to it."

How do all parts of the Bible fit together?

Let us consider how Revelation fits into the whole of God's Word. It is one thing to KNOW what God's Word says; to memorize it or to become intimately familiar with Bible passages. But it is another, and far more important thing, to understand how all of God's Word fits together, for only then will we understand its meaning and application to our lives.

God's Word is progressive and unfolding. God began with creation, and selected certain individuals thru whom He would speak ... Abraham, Isaac, Jacob (Israel), and then the people of Israel. So God moved from working thru select individuals to working thru an entire nation; Israel. But even then, it was His intent to bless all the peoples of the earth; all nations; thru Israel. (See Genesis 12:3; 22:18; 26:4-5; 28:14)

When Israel began to go astray God chose prophets to speak to the nation and to call her back to repentance and obedience. But continued rebellion led to exile. Still the prophets spoke and promised a restoration of the kingdom that had once been established by David. The people awaited this restoration and the promised Messiah who would bring the restoration.

In the gospel accounts the Messiah (Christ) comes, speaking of the nearness of the kingdom. This was the promise the people had been waiting for. But Christ was rejected by Israel, and as a result there was a delay in the kingdom's restoration. But in Acts the Twelve carry on with the same message. If the people would repent, Christ would return and there would be a restoration of the kingdom. (Acts 3:19-21) But still the people rejected Christ (Acts 28:26-28), and the kingdom was further delayed.

So, God did a new thing; an amazing thing. Setting aside Israel *temporarily* (Romans 11:25) He spoke directly to the nations thru a new apostle; Paul. Paul was not one of the Twelve, but was an ADDITIONAL apostle with a new mission, unheard of in the past. He would speak to the nations, introducing the Body of Christ consisting of Jew and Gentile alike with no barrier or preference. This created no small stir, for Israel was offended by this heretical message. (Acts 22:21-23) THEY were the people of God, not the nations.

While Paul proclaimed the message assigned to him (the evangel of the Uncircumcision per Galatians 2:7), Peter and the others continued with their message to Israel ... repent and the kingdom would be restored. Peter and the other Circumcision writers penned their letters to the Circumcision as they awaited the kingdom. Repent, have faith and good works, and persevere! Israel still awaited the kingdom's restoration. And Revelation is the fulfillment of what they waited for. Christ, the King, returns; the kingdom is established once again; and faithful Israel serves its place as Christ rules over all the nations.

But what happened to the Body of Christ?

Israel is mentioned time and again throughout Revelation, but whenever the nations are mentioned it is always negative. It is Israel as contrasted with the nations. Nowhere do we see "the church" or the Body of Christ. This shows us that somewhere along the way the Body of Christ was removed from the scene in order that the turbulent times could proceed, and Satan could lead the ultimate rebellion without being impeded by the Body of Christ or the holy spirit that filled them. We see this "removal" in 1 Thessalonians 4 when Christ sounds the trump, the dead in Christ rise, and the living in Christ rise to meet Him in the air. And the Body of Christ begins its commission of reigning in the heavens, for its expectation was always related to the celestials and not the earth. And then, sometime after this, Christ returns to the earth and restores the kingdom with faithful Israel reigning with Him.

The Body of Christ reigning in the heavens, and Israel reigning upon the earth, we enter the final phase of God's restoration process. All of life to this point has been a process, but now we get closer and closer to the final goal. Paul records this in 1 Corinthians 15 where we see death abolished, all subjected to Christ, and God becoming All in all.

So as we study Revelation we must remember its context. While it may be positioned as the final book in the Bible, it does not reveal to us the "final condition" of mankind. At the end of the book the process continues, and only in Paul's writings are we told of the conclusion; the consummation.

Today we live in an era of grace as revealed to us by the apostle Paul. God is conciliated to the world, not reckoning mankind's offenses to them. (2 Corinthians 5:19) But a day will come when God will take the next step in His plan to reconcile all to Himself. Grace will not reign in that future era, but judgment; for judgment is what it will take to bring the most stubborn and rebellious into the fold.

In that future era Christ's ambassadors (2 Corinthians 5:20) will be recalled, as is typically the case when conditions become perilous in the nations where ambassadors serve. War is about to be declared on the rebellious world.

Even today mankind seems to have not only forgotten God, but has lost all consciousness to His existence. He is shut out of their every thought. And in the future era described in Revelation, this will be true to the extreme!

The world wants peace and satisfaction *without* Christ. And while the world will not respond to Christ, they will receive the antichrist. Using Satan, God will send to mankind a strong deception that they should believe the lie. God wants mankind to acknowledge Him and the supremacy of His spirit. For some, the events described in Revelation are necessary to lead mankind to this conclusion. And so the bulk of this book records the waging of a brief but decisive war by God to recover a lost world.

The world today is filled with plans to redeem mankind. Peace conferences are planned with great hope. Democracy is promoted as the great deliverer of mankind. Band together all nations into one and wars will cease. But democracy is inadequate. Dictators, even the most charismatic and well-intentioned, are inadequate. No one is able! It is God's intention that man come to this realization and turn to Him; but throughout Revelation in the final ages upon this earth we see a rebellious mankind turn to any scheme or person other than God to accomplish peace and satisfaction without Him.

The Eons

To properly understand the events unfolding in Revelation one must know what the word *eon* (*aion* in the Greek) means. The inconsistent manner in which this word is translated has *hidden* much of God's truth that He intends to *reveal*.

Since *eon* is often translated "eternity" unless that rendering will absolutely not fit within any given context, we miss the fact that there are a number of individual eons, each with a beginning and an ending. We will look at this more comprehensively in the appendix, but for our understanding of Revelation it is important to understand the phrase *the eons of the eons*. This phrase clearly speaks of at least two eons (eons is plural) out of ALL of the eons. A study of this phrase will lead us to the conclusion that *the eons of the eons* refers to the final two eons. Much of the content found within Revelation is occurring in these final two eons. When we encounter the phrase *eonian life* in the Scriptures, often in the gospel accounts during the Lord's earthly visitation, this refers to life in these final two eons.

Three Days

Also necessary to our understanding is the meaning of several different "days" that are mentioned in the Scriptures.

Man's day (1 Corinthians 4:3) is the day in which we presently live, when God gives man free reign to learn what he is capable of accomplishing on his own.

In Revelation John came to be in the *Lord's Day*. Our religious traditions would tell us the *Lord's Day* refers to Sunday, the Christian Sabbath. But there is no Biblical warrant for this. The *Lord's Day*, also referred to as the *Day of the Lord*, is that day that will come when man's day comes to its conclusion. It will be a time of terrible trouble as described by the Old Testament prophets; and in great detail within Revelation. Joel and Zechariah have much to say about the *Lord's Day*, and their descriptions are much the same as what we see in Revelation.

Finally, when the *Day of the Lord* has concluded, having accomplished its purpose, we will see the *Day of God*. This phrase is not found in Revelation, but is used by Peter (2 Peter 3:12) to describe the destruction of the current earth and the creation of a new earth.

The Kingdom

Throughout the Old Testament we saw the development of God's kingdom upon the earth. It is Israel acting as God's agent, in contrast with the nations. But Israel is rebellious and experiences judgment, removal from the land, and then restoration. The final form of this kingdom will be seen when the Son, having accomplished the purpose assigned to Him, delivers up the kingdom to the Father, that God may be All in all. (1 Corinthians 15:28)

The prophets prior to Israel's exile speak of Christ's coming in humiliation and His coming in glory without discriminating between two separate events. Israel's dispersion and restoration are also spoken of without mention of a time period gap intervening.

But the prophets after the exile reveal a bit more, and these distinctions can be seen. Israel had not really changed with the first exile and return, and the prophets speak of a second destruction of the rebuilt Jerusalem. There would be *another* period of desolation, but also another advent of the Messiah; with Israel ransomed at last, triumphant in the promised kingdom.

At His first coming Christ is rejected by Israel, and Israel is rejected by Him. At His second coming He is accepted by Israel, and Israel is accepted by Him.

Ezekiel tells us of the times after the setting up of Christ's kingdom upon the earth. Israel is supreme over the nations, and they are restored as a people. The land is reapportioned among the tribes, God's sanctuary is in their midst, and the descendent of David rules over them.

Daniel

Daniel's prophecies are an important prerequisite for a proper understanding of Revelation; for Revelation is the crisis of all of Daniel's predictions. The kingdoms of Daniel's great metallic image have all passed into history except the last one.

✓ Babylon came to an end during Daniel's lifetime.
✓ The Medo-Persian reign continued until its defeat by,
✓ Alexander.

Daniel's fourth kingdom is not Rome, but will be an empire in the future that includes *all* nations and peoples and languages. The ten toes of Daniel's image correspond with the ten horns of the beast in Revelation. Daniel provides an earlier, less complete glimpse; for in Revelation we find that all characteristics of Daniel's four beasts appear in a single creature.

The "Heptads"

Daniel refers to 69 *"sevens"* (or *heptads*; periods of seven) and then a 70th *"seven."* If we consider the first 69 sevens, as measured by the moon (360 days per year) there were 173,880 days from the decree of Artaxerxes to restore and build Jerusalem, until the Lord's triumphal entry into Jerusalem. (Luke 19:35-40) This being the case we can infer that the final "seven" will consist of a literal seven-year period (2,523 days). This final heptad is what we see described in Revelation.

And in the middle of this 7-year period the covenant with Israel will be broken. Satan will take active control of human affairs, and he will demand worship by all of humanity. Up until this mid-way point of the final heptad the Jews will have been given the right to worship their God in the temple at Jerusalem, guaranteed by an international treaty. But after the mid-way point there will be the most ferocious assault upon the Jews ever known.

Not consecutive

Let us not assume the events recorded in Revelation are chronological throughout. As we see things unfold, a subsequent chapter will sometimes go back to review those things from a different perspective or to expand upon them.

Differing Interpretations

When it comes to prophecy, and especially the book of Revelation, there are a number of distinct, broad interpretations. G.K. Chesterton commented in *Orthodoxy, "Though St. John the Evangelist saw many strange monsters in his vision, he saw no creatures so wild as one of his own commentators."*

Years ago Jill and I participated in a couples Bible Study group, and at one point we decided to study Revelation. We thought a good approach might be to have each couple purchase a different commentary on the book, and as we discussed each chapter each could share thoughts from the commentary they had chosen. It didn't take long for us to see that interpretations and opinions were widely varied. Some believed the events of Revelation had already taken place in full. Others taught that these events would occur in the future. And as for the details of every part of Revelation, there was great disagreement. Yet each of these commentaries spoke with authority. While differing interpretations can be found for every part of the Bible, it is especially prevalent with Revelation.

My notes that follow represent my own current understanding, based on my studies. I will outline some of the broad, differing interpretations of Revelation. But, as always, I encourage you to study the Scriptures and to think for yourself. Think about what others (including myself) are saying, but never think any person is the authority. All human beings are fallible.

But let me say this. Regardless of one's interpretation of this book, our daily walk should not be affected. Some will say that those awaiting the Lord to come and snatch them away ("the rapture") are poor stewards of God's creation in this present world. This should not be the case. Paul, the apostle to the nations, always encouraged his audience to live a life worthy of their calling, and to work for the good of all. This is our mandate regardless of how we see the events of Revelation unfolding, past or future.

According to Mr. A. E. Knoch in "The Unveiling of Jesus Christ" (page 90), *"The primary function of prophecy is to interpret the times so that the people may know the mind of God and the conduct which will accord with His will. Prediction is but a part of the prophetic office."*

As for speculating on the many details within this prophetic book, consider these words of Sir Isaac Newton (1642-1727) from his "Observations on Daniel and the Apocalypse of John."

"The folly of interpreters has been to foretell times and things by this prophecy of the Revelation, as if God designed to make them prophets. By this rashness they have not only exposed themselves, but brought the prophecy also into contempt. The design of God was much otherwise. He gave this, and the prophecies of the Old Testament, not to gratify men's curiosities by enabling them to foreknow things, but that, after they were fulfilled, they might be interpreted by the event; and His own providence, not the interpreter's, be then manifested thereby to the world. For the event of things, predicted many ages before, will then be a convincing argument that the world is governed by Providence."

Let us now look at a few of the broad schools of interpretation of Revelation.

The Redemptive-Historical View

This view sees all of Revelation as a *symbolic* picturing of the battle between good and evil. The judgments refer repeatedly to the events of human history in every age, exhorting believers in every era to remain faithful through periods of suffering.

I believe that the flaw in this perspective is the failure to "rightly divide" God's Word as we are commanded to do (2 Timothy 2:15). If distinctions intended by God are ignored, then any part of Scripture can be applied (or misapplied) to any situation. Israel becomes the church. Prophecies are interpreted in any number of ways, as we see fit. In short, that which God reveals is replaced by that which man judges to be so.

The Historicist View

This view sees the seals, trumpets, and bowls as picturing the church in its successive eras. Isaac Newton stated in his "Observations Upon the Prophecies of Daniel & the Apocalypse of St. John," *"The predictions of things to come relate to the state of the Church in all ages."*

The symbolism refers to a series of events affecting the history of the church (e.g. the fall of the Roman Empire, the corruption of the popes, the Reformation, etc.). Christ's return is always seen as imminent.

This view, then, places the church as we see it today at the center of everything. It ignores the distinction between Israel and the church. Again, this is a failure to "rightly divide" the Scriptures as we are instructed to do.

The Preterist View

Preterism is the belief that the prophecies in Revelation have already been fulfilled in 70 A.D. A "full" or "consistent" preterist believes that ALL of Revelation has been fulfilled, while a "partial" preterist believes that MOST was fulfilled.

Partial preterists believe that God judged Israel, destroyed the temple, and ended the old covenant, but they still await the return of Christ to setup His kingdom on earth. They believe in a future resurrection.

To the Preterist, Babylon represents rebellious Israel which persecutes the church. But Babylon is never used in any ancient literature to refer to Israel. Some in this camp say that Babylon is the Roman Empire, and the prophecies in Revelation were fulfilled when that empire was destroyed in the fifth century.

A few of the Scriptural substantiations of this perspective according to authors taking the Preterist position:

Matthew 24:14 says, *"The gospel of the kingdom shall be preached in the whole world for a testimony unto all nations; and then shall the end come."* There are multiple passages in the epistles that tell us the gospel HAS been preached in the whole world. (Romans 1:8; 10:18; 16:26; 1 Thessalonians 1:5-7; Colossians 1:6; 1:23.) So, the prophecies in Revelation *must* have taken place shortly thereafter.

When Jesus says that *"this generation shall by no means pass away till all these things be fulfilled,"* (Matthew 24:34) he was referring to the generation of those that were then living. Matthew 10:23 says, *"Ye shall not have gone through the cities of Israel till the Son of Man be come."* For these words to be true, then, all must have taken place before that generation had died.

The apostles believed and proclaimed that the end times were near. (James 5:8; 1 Peter 4:7; John 2:18) How could the inspired writers, guided by the holy spirit, have been mistaken?

1 Peter 1:20 tells us, *"who was foreknown, indeed, before the foundation of the world, but <u>was manifested</u> at the end of the times for your sake."*

Historians record certain events that are fulfillments of prophecies. Josephus gives an account of the troubled times before the fall of Jerusalem. The peace that prevailed during Christ's lifetime was broken when the Roman armies overran Palestine ("blood flowed like water"), there was a great famine (AD 49) and a pestilence (AD 65).

When Peter speaks of the fiery flames that ushered in the new earth (2 Peter 3) this was the *symbolic* fire that Jesus had talked of in Luke 12:49. Neither Peter nor Paul associated Christ's coming with a <u>physical</u> change to the universe. The heaven and earth that would pass away, to be replaced with a new heaven and earth, were simply representative of the old and temporary covenant being replaced with the new covenant.

When Luke said, *"Make ye ready the way of the Lord. Make His paths straight. Every valley shall be filled, and every mountain and hill shall be brought low, and the crooked shall become straight,"* (Luke 3:5,6) he was speaking of a *moral* leveling and not the *physical* cutting down of mountains and hills.

The "Christian era" was the coming of the unseen inner kingdom, not only for a thousand years (the millennium) but forever. (2 Peter 1:11; Luke 1:33)

Preterist writers see the spread of Christianity bringing about the fullness of the kingdom. "It is by the influence of Christianity that we shall approach universal peace." (Benjamin Harrison) "Each generation leaves a better world than that into which it was born." (Bascom)

But from my observation of current events throughout the course of my lifetime, the world is getting worse; not better.

The Preterist view believes that the western mind tends to take *literally* language that was intended to be *figurative*. "The passing of heaven and earth" in Isaiah 13 was a figurative description of the passing of Babylon when they were defeated by the Medes. When

Isaiah 34 describes the dissolution of the earth and heavens it was a prediction of the fall of the Edomites. So, the Lord "came" with the fall of Babylon, Assyria, etc. There was a *spiritual* coming of Christ in 70 A.D. Jesus' statement about "coming on the clouds" was simply a *figurative* way to represent the majesty of God.

The Futurist View

This view sees all of Revelation, except for the letters to the churches, as the yet future return of Christ in the end times. Dispensational futurism interprets the visions very literally, chronologically unfolding the events to take place. Progressive dispensationalism holds to a looser, less literal approach. Many of the visions are interpreted symbolically. Some hold that the church is true Israel, and that there will be no pre-tribulation rapture. Christians will pass through the final period of trial.

For the most part, the order of events begins with the church being raptured into heaven, followed by a seven year tribulation period. The reign of antichrist begins, the nations gather to make war against Jerusalem, Christ returns and defeats the nations, Christ rules during the millennium, Satan gathers the rebellious unbelievers at the end of the millennium to fight against Christ, and Christ finally defeats Satan and begins his eternal reign.

There is much speculation. In every era of history interpreters have identified certain prominent individuals as the anti-christ. Hitler, Sadam Hussein, the pope (at various times) have all been identified, and then replaced with another when they disappear from the scene. Thus also various nations are identified with certain elements of Revelation, but are then replaced with other nations when the former fade from view. In short, the Bible is interpreted by modern events.

Dispensational Futurism

From my studies of the Scriptures I believe this to be the proper interpretation of that which God has revealed. But even within this camp there are improprieties, with speculation at times when the Scriptures are silent. It is here that care must be taken. We must rightly divide the Scriptures to see the distinctions in things God has intended to be distinct (e.g. Israel vs. the church). But we must also avoid speculating on things where God has chosen to remain silent. Our human nature is curious, and we want to know every detail. But there are times God has deemed certain details unnecessary to share, and perhaps irrelevant to the point He is wanting to reveal.

"That it is future, is all we know. No dates are given. God's reckonings are not by dates but by duration. Satan's craft is seen in getting men to fix dates; so that when the expected event does not transpire the subject may become one of ridicule and so the glorious hope has been made a subject of mockery." (William Tucker Broad, 1860-1923; Associate of E.W. Bullinger; Things to Come, May 1906)

Revelation

An Overview of the Scriptures, by
BOB EVELY © 2018.
An Independent Minister of Christ Jesus,
Of the church at Wilmore, Kentucky

"I am coming swiftly, and My wage is with Me, to pay each one as his work is." (22:12)

Revelation was written by the apostle John, probably in 96 A.D.; some 40 years after his three epistles were penned, and nearly 30 years after the last of Paul's epistles. So, all of the Scriptures had been finalized, and then a 30-year silence before this final writing.

As we begin our study of Revelation, let us recall these words from the apostle Paul ... *be learning not to be disposed above what is written.* (1 Corinthians 4:6) More than any other portion of God's Word, Revelation is the subject of great speculation. Many different authors, scholars, and teachers will tell us what every detail means. But since there is much disagreement among them, we should proceed with care. Let us consider that which is *revealed* to us, without speculating on those things which the Lord saw fit to leave less obvious.

CHAPTER 1

Opening (1:1)

The unveiling of Jesus Christ, which God gives to Him, to show to His slaves what must occur *swiftly*; and He signifies it, dispatching through His messenger to His slave John, who testifies ... whatever he perceived.

> The King James Version assigns the title, "The Revelation of St. John the Divine." But this is not the revelation, or unveiling, of St. John. It is "The Unveiling of Jesus Christ!" It is not a revelation only of things to come, but an unveiling of a person; Jesus Christ! It is a revelation given THRU John, but is an unveiling OF Jesus Christ.

> The Greek is *apokalupsis* from which we get our English *apocalypse*. Most translations render the word *revelation*. Things that have been concealed in the past are now *revealed* by God. The Concordant Version renders the word *unveiling*.

To the Believer in this present age, Jesus Christ has been *unveiled.* We recognize Him as Lord; as the Son of God. But to the world He remains veiled, ever since He departed earth and ascended into heaven following the resurrection. Furthermore, even to the Believer the things that are to take place in the future are *veiled* until God provides the *unveiling.* This He has done in His Word.

The book of Revelation records Christ's unveiling as it pertains to His return to the earth to reign. The tribulation to take place prior to Christ's return to the earth, and His long-awaited return, have been revealed to John and are recorded in this book.

We must remember that Paul also was given an *unveiling* that is found in the Scriptures. He did not simply learn "the gospel" from the Twelve. Paul received revelation directly from Christ. *"For neither did I accept it from a man, nor was I taught it, but it came through a revelation of Jesus Christ."* (Galatians 1:12)

Paul was an apostle; but he was not one of the Twelve. We recall from Acts 1 the importance of replacing Judas with one, returning the number of the apostles to twelve. Just as there were twelve tribes in Israel, and just as Jesus had appointed twelve apostles, so also the early church found it necessary to replace Judas with only <u>one</u> to return the number to twelve. But when Paul became an apostle it was not to maintain the number at twelve. Paul was in <u>addition</u> to the twelve. Why is this important?

The Twelve were Jews! They proclaimed the kingdom to be restored to ISRAEL as had been promised by the Old Testament prophets. *"Lord, art Thou at this time restoring the kingdom to Israel?"* (Acts 1:6) The Twelve were commissioned to go ONLY to the Jews; the *sheep of Israel.* (Matthew 10:5-7; 15:24; 19:28-29; Acts 2:22; 2:36; 4:10)

Paul's commission was different; *"... for he is a choice instrument of Mine, to bear My name before both the nations and kings, besides the sons of Israel."* (Acts 9:15-16)

> # John, the author of Revelation, was one of the Twelve, commissioned to go solely to Israel!

Paul was an apostle, but not one of the Twelve. He was commissioned to go not only to Israel, but also to the nations. And Paul did not simply study under the Twelve to learn the gospel; he was given revelation directly from Jesus Christ.

Christ revealed to Paul that which the Body of Christ could expect; to be "snatched away" to meet Christ in the air when the trumpet sounds. (1 Thessalonians 4:13-18)

Christ revealed to John that which ISRAEL could expect; for Christ to return to the earth, to restore the kingdom to Israel and to reign. This is what we read about in Revelation. Revelation is not about the expectation of the Body of Christ; Paul was commissioned to write about that. John is commissioned to write to Israel concerning *her* expectation. Pay close attention, and you will see many references to Israel throughout Revelation ... and no references to the Body of Christ.

What means have been employed by God to provide this unveiling? We read in the first verse that God gives the *unveiling* to Him (Christ), Who in turn shows these things to *His slaves*, through *His slave John.* John *testifies to the word of God and the testimony of Jesus Christ, whatever he perceived.*

So; John is permitted to *perceive* (to see) certain things; things he has been commanded to record. The book of Revelation is John's report.

So, Jesus Christ, Who had died and was resurrected and ascended into heaven, is now UNVEILED. John has been selected to receive God's revelation.

John will be shown things that *must occur* SWIFTLY. This is not necessarily *soon* after John received the revelation, but once the events begin they will unfold *swiftly.* In John 20:4 John and Peter start out together, but John runs more *swiftly* than Peter. Once they began, John's arrival at the tomb was *swift.*

One final observation before we move on. We are told at the onset that this revelation is to show Christ's slaves, or servants, what will occur. But the Body of Christ was told they were no longer servants, but sons. (Galatians 4:7) Throughout the Old Testament those of Israel are constantly spoken of as *servants.* But if Revelation speaks to or about the Body of Christ, why is there no mention of *sons* anywhere to be found?

Happy is he who is reading and those who are hearing the word of the prophecy, and who are keeping that which is written in it, *for the era is near.*

Near is conditional. Epaphroditus was *near* death, but he recovered. (Philippians 2:30) The Lord proclaimed that the kingdom was *near* during His earthly ministry, but it was not realized in short order because Israel rejected her king. Furthermore, the era may be *near* in God's timing, but to Him a day may be like a thousand years. (2 Peter 3:8)

The address on the envelope [(1:4)]
John; to the seven ecclesias which are in the province of Asia.

John, as one of the Twelve, always addressed the Jewish believers; never the nations. The ecclesias ("called-out-ones") in this case are the believers from among Israel.

BEWARE: Most Bible translations use "church" for ecclesia throughout Revelation. But the ecclesia John addressed was comprised exclusively of Israelite believers!

The "Chief" of the kings of the earth [(1:4)]

Grace to you and peace from Him Who is and Who was and Who is coming, and from the seven spirits which are before His throne,

And from Jesus Christ, the Faithful Witness, the Firstborn of the dead, and the *Suzerain* of the kings of the earth. To Him Who is loving us and looses us from our sins by His blood.

> Grand descriptions of the King Who is to come; the Lord Jesus Christ. He now resides in the heavens with seven spirits before His throne. But as this revelation to John will promise, He is coming.

> *Suzerain* is often translated *prince*. The Greek is *archon* which denotes *chief*. Jesus Christ is the *chief* of the kings of the earth, although these kings do not yet realize that. Until this time the earth is in the midst of *man's day*, (1 Corinthians 4:3) where kings believe *they* are the ultimate *chiefs*. But a new day; the *Lord's day* is coming, and this is the message that John brings.

And makes us a kingdom and priests to His God and Father, to Him be glory and might *for the eons of the eons.*

Observe the Jewish nature
of this book!

> To the Jews it was given to be *priests* unto God. *Priests* is not a term ever used of a Gentile, or of the Body of Christ. *Priests* always have to do with Israel and not the nations. As we proceed, look closely for the many references to Israel throughout Revelation. The content speaks to and of Israel and not the Body of Christ.

> *Eons of the eons* would be at least two eons (eons is plural) out of all of the eons (or ages). It is the last two eons that are spoken of here, when Christ reigns upon the earth. Christ will not reign "forever and ever" but only *for the eons of the eons,* UNTIL all is subjected to Him (1 Corinthians 15:25) and He completes the purpose God has assigned to Him, and He turns the kingdom over to the Father.

He is coming (1:7)

He is coming with clouds, and every eye shall be seeing Him.

> This passage comes from Zechariah 12:10. We see only Jew and Gentile; not the Body of Christ.
>
> There are those who believe that every prophecy and event described in Revelation was fulfilled and completed in the past, and that Christ has already returned to the earth; figuratively. But in my opinion this passage tells us He has not yet returned and the earth still awaits this event. For when He does come, every eye will see Him. There will be no confusion or question of His return. History has not, in my opinion, recorded this event!

The Alpha and Omega (1:8)

I am the Alpha and the Omega, is saying the Lord God, Who is and Who was and Who is coming, the Almighty.

> In the Old Testament we see the title *Elohim* (*God* in the Greek New Testament) and we see the name *Yahweh* (no equivalent in the Greek New Testament). But the name *Yahweh* comes from the Hebrew root words for *I Am* collectively in the past tense, present tense, and future tense. So, the equivalent in the Greek New Testament would be *Who is and Who was and Who is coming.*
>
> But does this mean Christ Jesus; the One described here Who is and Who was and Who is coming; is the same *being* as the God of the Hebrew Old Testament? I believe that Christ Jesus was the firstborn of creation, and that He was the "agent" for all creation that followed. I believe that much of what we see in the Old Testament is Christ Jesus the Son, acting as an agent for God the Father Who is behind the scenes and above all. So, while the terms "God the Father" and "Christ Jesus the Son" are not used in the Hebrew Old Testament; I believe we see both God the Father (Elohim in Genesis 1:1) and Christ Jesus the Son (Yahweh; the One Who is and Who was and Who is coming).

In the Lord's Day (1:9)

I, John ... came to be in the island called Patmos. I came to be, in spirit, *in the Lord's day.*

> John finds himself on the island of Patmos, where tradition tells us he was exiled. He is caused to be *in spirit* (as contrasted with *in flesh*).

One small word mistranslated can sometimes promote a major misunderstanding. John was not in the Spirit "on" the Lord's day. Instead, he found himself "in" the Lord's day. This verse has nothing to do with the day of the week on which John recorded this revelation. It has to do with the fact that while John lived (as we do) in man's day, in spirit he was permitted to be in *the Lord's day* (or *the day of the Lord*), and to record that which he was permitted to see.

What is "The Lord's Day?"

E. W. Bullinger wrote, "It is not a question of when John received this vision: but of what he saw in it. Whether it was a Sunday or Monday can have no real relation to the book. Our lot is cast in 'Man's day.' (1 Corinthians 4:3) Now is the time when man is judging; and few, if any, escape from experiencing sad proofs of the fact. But, thank God, 'man's day' will not go on forever. Another day is coming, and that will be 'the Lord's Day.' Then, He will be the judge."

This mistranslation has perpetuated the misconception that *the Lord's day* is Sunday, the "Christian sabbath." But the Bible speaks of no such thing as a Christian sabbath. The sabbath, being the seventh day, was given to the Jew to observe as a part of the law. In this present age there is no such day designated as *the Lord's day*. This is a fabrication of man's traditions. *The Lord's day* instead refers to a time not yet here, when *man's day* will cease and when *the Lord's day* will begin. To John it was given to experience *the Lord's day* that will occur in the future, enabling him to bring this revelation of Christ to mankind.

Many today are led to believe that *the Lord's day* refers to Sunday, for tradition teaches that Israel's Saturday Sabbath had become the Christian's Sunday Sabbath. But there is absolutely no Scriptural teaching of that sort. The Sabbath was only ever required of Israel, and it is only because Christians seek to *substitute* themselves for Israel throughout the Scriptures that we have this confusion.

There is no difference in meaning between the phrase *the Lord's day* and *the day of the Lord*. The linguistic difference relates only to emphasis.

The prophets emphasized the character of *the day* that was to come (the day of the Lord), while John emphasizes *the Lord* as He is unveiled and exalted (the Lord's day). The Scriptures speak often of the day of the Lord.

There are three distinct days mentioned in God's Word. Paul refers to our present day as *man's day* or *the day of man*. (1 Corinthians 4:3) This is a day to which Paul has no desire to conform. Man is judging. During this era man displays what he is not capable of accomplishing on his own. No matter what the circumstance, the form of government (even democracy) or the proliferation of well-intentioned laws, there is continued failure. Man's day will come to an end when *the day of the Lord* arrives, but it must last long enough to allow humanity to prove its inabilities. Thankfully, man's day will not go on forever.

The day of the Lord, into which John finds himself transported in his vision, is the time foretold by the prophets.

It seems that the common theme to each of these days is *exaltation*. Man has exalted himself in the day of man. When the Lord returns, He will be exalted in the day of the Lord. And God will be exalted on the new earth, in *the day of God*. (2 Peter 3:12)

So, to facilitate this revelation given to John, he is temporarily "transported" to this era called *the Lord's day* and he will see and record the events that will take place in that future day. By the spirit John saw the events that will take place in *The Day of the Lord*.

Tell the seven ecclesias (1:11)

I hear behind me a voice, loud as a trumpet, saying, What you are observing write into a scroll and send it to the seven ecclesias: to Ephesus and to Smyrna and to Pergamum and to Thyatira and to Sardis and to Philadelphia and to Laodicia.

In his *"Commentary on Revelation,"* E.W. Bullinger observes that in every part of the Bible the one object for many readers is to find the Church. There is no attempt to *rightly divide* the Word of God in accord with 2 Timothy 2:15. It is assumed that all of the Bible speaks directly to us in our present day and situation. But ...

> # Today's church is not the subject of Revelation!

Instead we see God's final dealings with the Jew and the nations; not the Body of Christ. Throughout we see Jewish imagery; the Temple, the Tabernacle, the Ark of the Covenant, the Altar, the Incense, the Priests. All of this belongs to Israel, not the Body of Christ which is conspicuously absent.

The Body of Christ today is waiting to be received up in glory. (1 Timothy 3:16) We await our calling on high. (Philippians 3:14) We look for Christ to change these mortal bodies into a glorious body like His own. (Philippians 3:20,21) And with the Body of Christ nowhere to be found in Revelation it would seem that all of these things will take place before the opening of Revelation.

There are various theories concerning the seven *ecclesias*, most often translated "churches," to whom these letters are addressed. Some say these are seven different *kinds* of ecclesias that represent the many other ecclesias in that day. Others say these seven ecclesias represent the various kinds of churches, good and bad, in our present day. Or perhaps these are seven specific ecclesias that *will* exist at the opening of the Lord's Day that John now observes.

Regardless, while we can certainly learn from the letters directed to these seven ecclesias as to behaviors and attitudes that God approves of and that which God does not approve of; we must be careful not to see these letters speaking directly to us in our present day. As we will see, these ecclesias are comprised exclusively of believers from among Israel.

John looks for the voice that spoke to him. He sees seven golden lampstands, and in their midst is One like a son of mankind with a voice like the sound of many waters. In His right hand are seven stars, and out of His mouth a sharp two-edged blade. His countenance is as the sun.

This description of the son of man is much like Daniel's vision. (Daniel 10:5)

In Hebrews 4:12 the word of God is described as a double-edged sword. It is the word of God that proceeds from the mouth of this Son of Mankind.

E. W. Bullinger notes that *the son of man* is a title that always refers to the Lord Jesus in connection with His dominion in the earth. "And, when used of His second coming, it refers to the judgment which He is then and there to exercise. While it occurs 84 times in the New Testament, it is never once used in the Pauline epistles addressed to Churches; thus proving that this title has nothing whatever to do with the Church." Revelation is focused on the coming of the Son of Mankind to exercise judgment and to assume dominion over the earth.

John falls at His feet, but is told, Do not fear! I am the First and the Last, and the Living One: And I became dead, and lo I am living for the eons of the eons. I have the keys of death and of the unseen. Write what you perceived, and what they are, and what is about to be occurring after these things.

These things that "*are*" will be viewed from John's perspective in the midst of his experiences. So, these things that *are* will be future events since John's vision is of a time in the future.

The secret of the seven stars and the seven lampstands. The seven stars are *messengers* of the seven ecclesias, and the seven lampstands are seven ecclesias.

The seven lampstands should cause us to recall the lampstand in the Tabernacle in Exodus 25. There we saw one lampstand with seven lamps. But now scattered, Israel is here represented by seven lampstands. As one lampstand represented Israel in unity, seven lampstands represents Israel in dispersion.

A *messenger* (*angelos* in the Greek) can be either an angelic being or a human being. Both can be found in the Scriptures, and only the context can tell us if a messenger is an angel or a human. *Messenger* refers to the being's mission, not its composition.

In the present context we ask; what purpose would there be in directing letters to angels? Furthermore, within a synagogue there is a *messenger* or legate that ranks directly below the chief of the synagogue. He is the mouthpiece of the congregation. So, it appears that these letters to the seven ecclesias are directed to this mouthpiece of each congregation. And this displays once again that

> # It is Israel, with its synagogues and messengers, that is the focus of Revelation.

So, John is instructed to write that which he will see; and what these things are (i.e. their meaning), and the things that will be occurring. But how will John know what the things he sees are, or what they mean? Here we see that John will be told what these things mean, if God determines he should know. There is no need for John to speculate. The things he is told to write to the ecclesias will be made clear to him.

We should take a lesson from this. There is much speculation about the meaning of every detail within Revelation. But we should not presume to know with certainty the meaning of things not clearly revealed. Let us simply rejoice in the knowledge provided clearly within the Word itself.

CHAPTER 2

To the ecclesia in Ephesus (2:1)

Commendations: Acts, toil, endurance, refusal to bear evil men, trying and finding false those saying they are apostles who are not, bearing because of My name and not being wearied, hating the acts of the Nicolaitans which I also hate.

Criticisms: Leaving your first love.

Charge: Remember whence you have fallen, repent, and do the former acts.

Warning: If not I am coming to you and will remove your lampstand.

> Ephesus was the capital and largest city in Asia. It is in the present-day Turkey. It was a very immoral city. An ecclesia was established there (Acts 19) and Paul devoted more time there than at the other ecclesias. (Acts 20:31)

But it would seem that these letters pertain to the ecclesias not as they were in the days of the apostles, but as they will be in the Lord's Day; for that is what John is seeing and describing.

> # Compare this letter to the Ephesians with Paul's letter to the Ephesians.

Is there any similarity? Paul's letter is on such a high plane; with spiritual promises and expectations; and rooted purely in grace and not law. Not so with this letter to the Ephesians recorded by John. Why? I contend that the Body of Christ has been removed from the scene before the events of Revelation begin to unfold. The age of grace has ended. God once again works with and thru Israel, under a covenant of law.

The words "*to him that overcometh*" are foreign to Paul. The Body of Christ has already overcome *in Him*. They are already more than conquerors. John, too, in his New Testament epistles notes that those within the ecclesia have already overcome. But those being addressed here in Revelation are living in a different era. This is the era of the beast, and great tribulation. The call to those living in this future era is to overcome, and to endure to the end.

The Nicolaitans are not found in any historical record. Perhaps this is because no such cult existed in history, but will in this future era. In the original language the word Nicolaitans is comprised of two words, "conquer-people," and would therefore seem to pertain to conquerors of some kind. When the first seal is opened we will see a rider on a white horse coming forth to conquer. (6:2) This is the false Messiah. The Nicolaitans could perhaps be those from among Israel that follow the false Messiah and worship the wild beast; false teachers who attempt to usurp the authority of the apostles.

To the ecclesia in Smyrna (2:8)

Commendations: Acts, affliction, poverty (though you are rich), bearing the calumny of those saying they are Jews but are not; but are a synagogue of Satan.

Criticisms: None.

Charge: Fear nothing you are about to be suffering. The Adversary is about to cast some of you into jail to be tried, and you will have affliction ten days. Become faithful until death and I will give you the wreath of life. The one who is conquering will not be injured by the second death.

Warning: None

> Smyrna was a port city; the present-day Ismia, Turkey. Here there were many Jews who opposed the ecclesia and the evangel.
>
> *Ten days of affliction* are probably that which is seen with the fifth seal. (6:9) This horrific, intense persecution of the faithful Jews will last ten days. The wreath or crown of life could be a reference to the annual athletic games, where Smyrna was a key participant.
>
> Observe the reference to those saying they are Jews, and who are obviously speaking poorly (with calumny) of those in the ecclesia who by inference are truly JEWS. And observe the reference to *the synagogue of Satan.*

These references show us it is ISRAEL that is being addressed and not the Body of Christ.

> When has it ever been a requirement to "profess to be Jews" to enter the ecclesia of today; the Body of Christ?

To the ecclesia in Pergamum (2:12)

Commendations: You dwell where the throne of Satan is, and you hold to My name and do not disown My faith in the days when Antipas, My faithful witness, was killed.

Pergamum was a great religious center, and an intellectual center. It boasted a huge library, and was the first location of a temple dedicated to Caesar.

Observe that in the Day of the Lord there will be a specific place where Satan's throne will be setup in this world, and where he and the beast will receive worship. This has always been Satan's objective.

Criticisms: You have those holding to the teaching of Balaam, who taught Balak to cast a snare before the sons of ISRAEL, to eat idol sacrifices and commit prostitution. You also have those holding to the teaching of the Nicolaitans.

Balaam was a prophet who prostituted himself. (Numbers 22-25)

Again we see mention of *the sons of Israel.* Clearly these words are being directed exclusively to the believers from within Israel, not the Body of Christ.

Charge: Repent.

Warning: If you do not repent I am coming to you swiftly and will be battling them with the blade of My mouth.

Blessing: To the one who is conquering I will be giving of the hidden manna, and a white pebble upon which a new name is written, of which no one is aware except the one obtaining it.

The white pebble was used when allotting the land. Each man's name was written on a pebble and they were placed in a bag and drawn for each parcel of land to be assigned. So here the white pebble will be an earnest of their kingdom allotment. And this all pertains to Israel, not the Body of Christ.

To the ecclesia in Thyatira (2:18)

Commendations: Acts, love, faith and service, endurance, your last acts are more than the former.

Criticisms: I have much against you. You pardon Jezebel who says she is a prophetess and is teaching and deceiving My slaves to commit prostitution and to eat idol sacrifices. I give Jezebel time that she should repent, but she is not willing to repent of her prostitution.

Warning: I will cast her and those committing prostitution with her into great affliction if they will not repent of her acts. I will be giving to each of you in accord with your acts.

Blessing: To those who refuse Jezebel's teaching and who do not know the deep things of Satan as they are saying, I will cast no other burden on you.

Charge: Hold what you have until I arrive.

Promise: To those who are conquering and keeping my acts until the consummation, I WILL BE GIVING AUTHORITY OVER THE NATIONS, and he will be shepherding them with an iron club as vessels of pottery are crushed.

> # Here we see clearly that the message is being given to ISRAEL!

Thyatira was the least important of the seven cities politically. It was a trade center with many trade guilds.

Those faithful within the Jewish ecclesia (called-out-ones) will have authority over the nations when Christ returns. Israel will serve as Christ's right hand in bringing those of the nations into subjection.

It is interesting that Tertullian and Epiphanius say there was no ecclesia in Thyatira when John wrote. But remember, John has been "transported" to a future day; *the Day of the Lord;* and in that day there will be an ecclesia at this place.

CHAPTER 3

To the ecclesia in Sardis (3:1)

Commendations: You have a few who do not pollute their garments.

Criticisms: You have a name and are living, and are dead. Your acts are not completed in the sight of God.

Charge: Become watchful and establish those who are about to be dying. Remember how you have obtained. Keep it and repent.

Warning: If you should not be watching, I will arrive on you as a thief. You will not know the hour I shall arrive.

Promise: Those that do not pollute their garments shall walk with Me in white, for they are worthy. The one who is conquering shall be clothed in white garments and his name will not be erased from the scroll of life, and I will be avowing his name before My Father and His messengers.

> Sardis was a wealthy and wicked city; the home of King Croesus and Aesop. It was a manufacturer of woolen garments.
>
> We within the Body of Christ are unworthy in ourselves, but worthy in Christ. But in this future era one will be worthy based on their own merit; their *overcoming* and *remaining faithful* to the end.
>
> The *scroll of life* is mentioned six times in Revelation. It consists of the names of those who do not worship the wild beast (chapters 13 and 17). The scroll (or book) is also mentioned in the Old Testament, always in conjunction with the people of Israel. (See, for example, Daniel 12:1; Deuteronomy 29:18-20.) The scroll was kept in the Temple and contained the registry of the lineage for Israelites.

To the ecclesia in Philadelphia [3:7]

Commendations: You have little power, and you keep My word and do not disown My name. You keep the word of My endurance.

Criticisms: None.

Promise: I am aware of your acts, and have granted an open door before you that no one is able to lock. Those of the synagogue of Satan who are saying they are Jews and are not, they will be arriving and worshiping before your feet. They will know that I love you. Seeing that you keep the word of My *endurance*, I will be keeping you out of the hour of trial which is about to be coming on the whole inhabited earth, to try those dwelling the earth.

> Philadelphia is the modern-day Alasehir, Turkey.

> # Observe that those "of the synagogue of Satan" are not lost forever!

Once the kingdom is restored with Christ reigning on the throne, those outside the city (including those "of the synagogue of Satan" as we see here) will enter to worship. And there they will see those of faithful Israel serving the King within the city.

The faithful ones did not deny His name by receiving another name (the beast). Endurance is key in this day of distress. It is mentioned seven times in Revelation. And we recall from the gospel accounts, *He that endures to the end will be saved.* (Matthew 10:22; 24:13; Mark 13:13)

Warning: I am coming swiftly. Hold what you have that no one may be taking your wreath.

Promise: The one conquering I will be making a pillar in the temple of My God. I will write on him the name of My God and the name of the city of My God, the new Jerusalem, which is descending out of heaven.

We will see *the new Jerusalem* descending out of heaven in chapter 21.

To the ecclesia in Laodicea [3:14]

This says the Amen, the Faithful and True Witness, and God's creative Original.

Christ is described as *God's creative Original!* Not God Himself. *A* God but not *THE* God. *God's creative Original.* The very first of creation, and the foremost.

Commendations: None.

Criticisms: Acts, you are neither cool nor zealous, indifferent (so I am about to spew you out of My mouth), you say you are rich and in need of nothing but you are wretched, forlorn, poor, blind, and naked.

Charge: Buy from Me gold refined by the fire that you should be rich; and white garments that you may be clothed, and the shame of your nakedness may not be made manifest, and eye-salve to anoint your eyes that you may be observing. Whoever I am fond of I expose and discipline. So be zealous and repent.

Promise: I stand at the door and am knocking. If any should hear My voice and open the door, I will be coming in to him and dining with him. The one who is conquering will be seated with Me on My throne as I also conquer and am seated with My Father on His throne.

Laodicea was a very wealthy trade center, and the ecclesia shared in this wealth. It was known for its production of eye salve.

Consider these seven letters directed to the seven ecclesias.

As we consider all seven letters we observe that the people to whom they are addressed are expected to be well versed in the Jewish history of the Old Testament; all that had been written to their fathers. Each of the promises is conditioned; *to him that overcometh*. We find this same condition in the gospels and the Circumcision letters where faith plus works (enduring to the end) are requirements. But the concept is foreign to the language found in Paul's letters where salvation is by faith alone.

Observe also that none of these promises can be realized by the Body of Christ, for they all fall into a sphere that is not pertinent to our expectation. Our expectation lies in the heavens, the celestial realm; but everything mentioned in these letters is concerned with an expectation in the kingdom to be restored upon the earth. The bottom line;

The difference between these letters and the New Testament epistles (letters) is significant.

It is impossible to see how these Revelation letters that are steeped in works could harmonize with the Body of Christ that is under grace and not law.

Just as Paul wrote nine letters to seven different ecclesias, intended to be read by all, here we have seven letters directed to seven different ecclesias that will exist in the Day of the Lord. These letters provide a clear picture of Israel's condition in these ends times.

Seven "churches" or seven ecclesias?

Most Bible versions translate this "seven churches," and most today interpret John's writings as being directed to the churches of our day. But *ecclesia* does not always refer to the church! *Ecclesia* in Acts 19:32,41 for example, is clearly not the church, but a mob of citizens. In Acts 19:40 *ecclesia* is a court of law. In Acts 7:38 *ecclesia* is an assembly of people in the wilderness in Moses' day, long before the formation of "the church." Check these passages in your favorite Bible translation and you will see another word used besides "church."

So, *ecclesia* does not always mean "church." The Greek word is "ek" (out) "klesia" (called ones). The "out-called-ones" denote a specific group of people that are "called out" from, or distinguished from, a larger group of people.

Even when referring to those "called out" by God, the group being referred to is not always the same. For example, the *ecclesia* of Acts 5:11 should not be confused with the *ecclesia* of today, for in that day the called-out-ones were comprised exclusively of Jews. Gentiles were not eligible. In Acts 2:36 Peter speaks to *the house of Israel.* This is also clear in Acts 4:10; 5:31 and 11:19. The apostles preached only to the Israelites, and those of Israel who believed were a part of the *ecclesia* (those "called-out" in that day). But this is not the *ecclesia* that Paul spoke of, comprised of Jews and Gentiles without distinction, also known as the Body of Christ.

So those "called out" by God; the *ecclesia*, may be different groups in different instances.

We must "rightly divide" the scriptures.

The problem is that most Bible teachers fail to distinguish between things that are different in Scripture. They do not "rightly divide" or "correctly cut" the word of truth. (2 Timothy 2:15) Bible translators have also been influenced by these Bible teachings. They fail to distinguish between things that are different; often translating several different Greek words into a single English equivalent, thereby hiding the distinction God has made from the Bible student. And they often take a single Greek word and separate it into several different English words, often with significantly different meanings; also hiding the true meaning conveyed in the original language.

Ecclesia ... or church?

The Greek *ecclesia* is sometimes translated church, sometimes mob, sometimes assembly. When *church* seems to fit the context (as the translator understands the *church*), then *church* is the word we find in the translation. And we are led to believe that whenever *church* is found in the translation it is always referring to the same group; the church we know today.

In effect, our Bible translation has become an <u>interpretation</u> by those producing the translation! Translators have defined *church* for us. But as we have seen, *ecclesia* simply refers to a group of "called out ones," and this could be comprised of a different group from one instance to the next. Can we really trust the translators of the Bible version we have chosen as they define the *church* for us?

Again, there is a big difference between the *church* we see in Acts which is wholly comprised of Israelites, and the church that Paul speaks of which is comprised of Jew and Gentile alike with no distinction.

Consider the *church* in the book of Acts:

"Men! Israelites! Hear these words..."(Acts 2:22)

"Let all the house of Israel know..."(Acts 2:36)

"Those indeed, then, who are dispersed from the affliction which is occurring over Stephen, passed through as far as Phoenicia and Cyprus and Antioch, speaking the word to no one except to Jews only."(Acts 11:19)

Later in Acts, Paul announces he will turn to those of the nations, since Israel had rejected the gospel. *To you first was it necessary that the word of God be spoken. Yet, since, in fact, you are thrusting it away, and are judging yourselves not worthy of eonian life, lo! we are turning to the nations.* (Acts 13:46)

But even then, Paul would go first to the synagogues to address the Israelites.

"... they came to Thessalonica, where there was a synagogue of the Jews. Now, as was Paul's custom, he entered to them, and on three sabbaths he argues with them from the scriptures ..."(Acts 17:1)

"Now he argued in the synagogue on every sabbath ..."(Acts 18:4)

"Now it occurred three days after, that he calls together those who are foremost of the Jews."(Acts 28:17)

Until, at the very end of Acts, Paul announces:

"Let it be known to you, then, that to the nations was dispatched this salvation of God, and they will hear."(Acts 28:28)

We remember that Paul was *entrusted with the evangel of the Uncircumcision, according as Peter of the Circumcision ...* (Galatians 2:7) We have observed that through the book of Acts those receiving the Word of God were those of Israel. This makes perfect sense, since the message being proclaimed pertained to the kingdom that would be restored unto Israel as promised by the prophets of old. *Repent, then, and turn about for the erasure of your sins, so that seasons of refreshing should be coming from the face of the Lord, and He should dispatch the One fixed upon before for you, Christ Jesus, Whom heaven must indeed receive until the times of restoration of all* ... (Acts 3:19)

Israel awaited the coming of the Messiah who would reign on David's throne, restoring the kingdom to Israel. And thru Israel, all nations would be blessed. This was the message proclaimed to the ecclesia by Peter and the Twelve. And the ecclesia were Jewish believers.

But consider the ecclesia that Paul spoke of:

For there is no distinction between Jew and Greek ... (Romans 10:12)

Yet all the members of the one body, being many, are one body, thus also is the Christ. For in one spirit also we all are baptized into one body, whether Jew or Greeks, whether slaves or free, and all are made to imbibe one spirit. (1 Corinthians 12:12)

For whoever are baptized into Christ, put on Christ, in Whom there is no Jew nor yet Greek, there is no slave nor yet free, there is no male and female, for you all are one in Christ Jesus. (Galatians 3:27)

Peter, having been entrusted with the evangel of the Circumcision, spoke to the ecclesia comprised of believers out of Israel. Paul, having been entrusted with the evangel of the Uncircumcision, spoke to the ecclesia comprised of believers out of the nations. He later taught, in his letters, concerning the Body of Christ; comprised of Jew and Gentile without distinction.

Should we be mixing these *ecclesias* together, assuming they are the same? Would it not be better to simply transliterate the Greek *ekklesia* as *ecclesia* in our Bible translations, allowing the Bible student to discern from each instance who the *called out ones* are?

Now let us return to our present context.

When John writes to *the seven ecclesias* these are not seven *churches* as we would define churches today. If we pay close attention to the details we will see that these are seven *Jewish* ecclesias of the future *Day of the Lord* that John is permitted to see in this Unveiling; a day *still* future in this present age; when Christ will return to the earth to reign upon His throne. The Body of Christ (*church* as it exists today) is absent from Revelation.

What are the evidences in Revelation that lead us to believe the ecclesias John wrote to are <u>Jewish</u> ecclesias?

1:6 *"... makes us a kingdom and priests."* "Priests are always associated with Israel as they serve as God's instrument. We have direct access to the Father and need no priest to hinder our approach. But when the promised kingdom is restored Israel will serve God in His temple, and the other nations will be subordinate and will approach God thru them. "You [Israel] shall become *a kingdom of priests and a holy nation."* (Exodus 19:6)

2:1 *"To the messenger of the ecclesia ..."* Nowhere do we read of the ecclesias that are the Body of Christ (in Paul's writings) having a messenger associated with them. But historical writings do speak of messengers being associated with a synagogue.

2:9 *"... the calumny of those saying that they themselves are Jews, and they are not, but are a synagogue of Satan."* Here we see direct references associated strictly with Israel.

2:14 Note the reference to Balaam casting a snare before *"the sons of Israel."* Again; a direct reference to Israel.

2:17 *"... new name ..."* We note the connection to Israel when examining Isaiah 62:2 and 65:15.

2:27 To the one conquering is promised *"authority over the nations."* Throughout; "nations" is contrasted to Israel. ("Nations" is clearly not the Body of Christ.)

In his *"Commentary on Revelation"* E. W. Bullinger writes: "It is not only Hebrew in character as to its linguistic peculiarities, but especially in its use of the Old Testament ... All who know anything of Old Testament history cannot fail to detect the almost constant reference to it." [pg. 5]

But where is the church as we know it today in Revelation?

If John is writing to Jewish ecclesias in Revelation, where is the Body of Christ; "The Church" of our day? We see a number of references to Israel (3:9 for example), but no reference to the Body of Christ. Why?

We observe in 1 Thessalonians 4:13-18 that the Body of Christ awaits the Lord's call, at which point the dead and living in Christ will be snatched away *to meet the Lord in the air*. This must have occurred prior to the events John describes in Revelation, where we see *the Jewish ecclesia* upon the earth awaiting the Lord's coming to reign.

The Body of Christ awaits the Lord to call it upwards to be with Him. The ecclesia in Revelation, comprised of believing Israelites, awaits the Lord (Messiah) to return to the earth to reign.

Throughout the Old Testament God's chosen people were the Israelites. With the Body of Christ removed from the scene in the end times, once again we see Israel assuming that role. Israel was not to be "calloused" forever, but only *UNTIL the complement of the nations may be entering.* (Romans 11:25) And then, as prophesied in Isaiah 59:20-21, the Rescuer will turn Israel away from her irreverence. (Romans 11:26)

John writes to the seven ecclesias; the "out-called" of ISRAEL; in Asia.

CHAPTER 4

A door opens in heaven [(4:1)]
I saw a door open in heaven, and a voice as a trumpet said to me, Come up here and I will show you what must be occurring after these things. Immediately I came to be in spirit.

> # John is about to walk thru this door to perceive things that will occur in the Day of the Lord.

John is made to be "in spirit," perhaps similar to the day he will receive an incorruptible body, but for now only temporarily. He is about to see events that are to take place in the future.

In heaven ... the throne (4:2)

There was a throne upon which One is sitting. Around the throne were 24 thrones upon which elders were sitting, clothed in white garments and with golden wreaths on their heads. Out of the thrones issued lightnings and voices and thunders. Before the throne burn seven torches of fire, which are the seven spirits of God. And before the throne is a glassy sea.

This moment in the Day of the Lord is described in Psalm 103:19. *The Lord hath prepareth His throne in the heavens, and His kingdom ruleth over all.* Psalms 9, 10 and 11 foretell the scenes John describes in Revelation. Daniel 7:9-10 also speaks of this moment when, *I beheld till the thrones were set.*

The elders are the heads of the heavenly priesthood. *Elder* or *presbyter* is a title of honor and respect. It implies authority and maturity, not necessarily age.

> # Observe that the visions John describes will alternate between heaven and earth.

That which he sees on earth is the carrying out of the vision he had previously seen in heaven.

In the center of the throne and around the throne are four animals with eyes in front and behind. One is like a lion, another like a calf, a third with a face like a human, and the fourth like a flying vulture. Each has six wings, with eyes around and inside. Without resting day and night they proclaim: Holy, holy, holy, Lord God Almighty. Who was, Who is, and Who is coming.

> This is the same description as the cherubim in Ezekiel 1:10. It was cherubim that guarded the Garden of Eden.

Whenever the animals give glory and honor and thanks to the One sitting on the throne, the 24 elders also fall before Him and worship Him saying, You are worthy O Lord, *for you created all.*

> God's *creation* is the subject of these words of worship. Coming is the end of creation's groaning and travailing. (Romans 8:22)

CHAPTER 5

The lamb and the scroll (5:1)

The One seated on the throne has in His right hand a scroll, sealed with seven seals. A messenger asks: Who is worthy to open the scroll? No one in heaven or earth is able to open it. As I lamented one of the elders says, Do not lament. He conquers. The Lion of the tribe of Judah is to open the scroll.

The Lord is about to receive the title deed to the earth.

> The *scroll* is not a book, but a legal document (Matthew 19:7; Mark 10:4), much like a title, deed or mortgage. In this case it appears to be the title deed to the earth.

I saw a Lambkin standing, as though slain. It had seven horns and seven eyes which are the seven spirits of God, commissioned for the entire earth. It came and took the scroll, and the four animals and 24 elders fall before the Lambkin singing, You are worthy to take the scroll and open the seals. You were slain and buy us with your blood.

You make a kingdom and priesthood for our God out of every tribe and people and nation, and they shall be reigning on the earth.

> The kingdom and priesthood are comprised of Jews that have been scattered among the nations. Only those of Israel are ever referred to as a priesthood.
>
> Though the Lion of the tribe of Judah is the conqueror, John sees Him as a Lambkin that had been slain. Christ's first victory or conquering was when He prevailed as the Lambkin that was slain. A lambkin is a young lamb. It pictures weakness, as contrasted with the Lord's characterization as a lion and the mighty works He will perform.

I hear the sound of many messengers around the throne saying, Worthy is the Lambkin slain, to get power and riches and wisdom and strength and honor and glory and blessing. And I hear every creature in heaven and on the earth and under the earth and on the sea say, To Him Who is sitting on the throne and to the Lambkin be blessing and honor and glory and might for the eons of the eons.

> # Now as the seals are removed from the title deed, there will be great repercussions upon the earth. The Lord is preparing to take possession of what is His.

CHAPTER 6

The seals [(6:1)]

Seal #1 is opened: I see a white horse. Its rider has a bow, and a wreath is given to him. He comes forth conquering.

> When Daniel recorded his visions he was instructed to seal them. But the subject of Revelation is the unsealing. When it comes time for the fulfillment of the events described in Revelation, THEN the seals will be opened. And even then, as the seals are opened, there are things John must "seal up," such as the things uttered by the seven thunders. (10:4)

Now compare the first seal with Matthew 24:5. The false christ here in the first seal is an imitation of the real Christ. This is not the true Christ/Messiah. Matthew 24:5 foretold this; *For many shall be coming in My name, saying, 'I am the Christ!' and shall be deceiving many.* This rider on the white horse is an imitation of the true One, conquering the nations to unite them against God; and leading them to believe that he is the man of destiny able to solve humanity's problems and usher in the longed-for millennium.

Ezekiel 38-39 precedes this. Israel is protected supernaturally from an invasion from the north. The temple is rebuilt. And in 2 Thessalonians 2:6-12 the restrainer is removed that was holding back lawlessness (the Body of Christ with the spirit of God dwelling within). Now there is no longer a significant voice for morality and righteousness in the world.

Seal #2 is opened: There comes forth a fiery-red horse. To its rider is given to take peace out of the earth, that they should be slaying one another. He is given a large sword.

Compare this with Matthew 24:6. *You shall be about to be hearing of battles, and tiding of battles. Nation shall be roused against nation.*

All of Micah 7 seems to describe the period of this second seal, as does Daniel 11:33; *They shall fall by the sword, and by flame, by captivity, and by spoil, many days.*

Seal #3 is opened: There comes a black horse, and its rider has a pair of balances. A voice says, A choenix of wheat a denarius, and three choenix of barley a denarius, and the oil and wine you should not injure.

Compare this with Matthew 24:7. *There shall be famines and quakes.* A choenix of wheat (1.5 pints) will cost a denarius, which the Lord considered to be a day's wage. (Matthew 20:9-11) So all one will be able to do will be to earn food for himself. The usual price for a choenix of wheat was about one-eighth of a denarius, and sometimes much less. History records no scarcity this severe. Olive oil, wine and grain were the staple diet in ancient Palestine.

Famines will occur from secondary causes by which we tend to explain things. But the primary cause of these famines is a command from the throne.

Seal #4 is opened: There comes a greenish horse Its rider is named Death, and the Unseen follows him. He is given jurisdiction over a fourth of the earth to kill with the blade and with famine and with death and by the wild beasts of the earth.

> In Matthew 24:7b-8 death was prophesied.
>
> The first four seals correspond with the opening of the Olivet Discourse found in Matthew 24-25, Mark 13, and Luke 21. Where can we find any period in history where the judgments described in the first four seals has taken place in such great magnitude, and over one-fourth of the earth?

Seal #5 is opened: I see under the altar the souls of those who have been slain because of the word of God and their testimony. They cry with a loud voice, Till when, O Owner, will You not judge and avenge our blood? Each is given a white robe, and they are told to rest a little longer, until the number should be completed.

> Compare this with Matthew 24:9; martyrs! In Luke 18:1-8 the Lord describes His servants in these days; waiting and praying. Their cry for vengeance is identical with what we see here in the fifth seal.
>
> As we rightly divide God's Word to understand how He is working in various eras, we note that these cries for vengeance are foreign to the Body of Christ living in this current era of grace.

Seal #6 is opened: A great cataclysm. The sun becomes black; the moon as blood. The stars fall on the earth. Every mountain and island are moved out of place, and the kings of the earth, the magnates, the captains, the rich, the strong, and every slave and freeman hide themselves in caves and in the rocks of the mountains. They cry out for the rocks to hide them from the face of the One sitting on the throne, and from the indignation of the Lambkin, for the day of their indignation has come, and who is able to stand?

> In Matthew 24:10-13 chaos was prophesied. The sun turning black had been foretold in Joel 2:30-31; Zephaniah 1:15; Isaiah 13:9-10; and Isaiah 34:4. Joel had foretold that before the great and terrible Day of the Lord the sun would be turned to darkness and the moon to blood. (Joel 2:31; Acts 2:20)

Paul had reported that a day of indignation would come. (Romans 2:5) The events of that day are now being shared with John.

Consider Matthew 24:30. The Son of Man appears immediately after this great cataclysm. This sixth seal takes us to the same point as the seventh trumpet we will read of in chapter 11. So, the visions to follow are a review of the period already covered by these seals, with additional details provided and from a different perspective.

To recap the first six seals ...

Matt 24	Seal #		Rev 6
4,5	1	False christ	1,2
6,7	2	Wars	3,4
7	3	Famines	5,6
7	4	Pestilences	7,8
8-28	5	Martyrdoms	9-11
29-30	6	Signs in heaven of advent	12-17

Some believe the sixth seal was fulfilled at the conversion of Constantine and the overthrow of paganism. But at that time there was no convulsion of nature in heaven or upon the earth. There was no fleeing to the mountains or cries of terror.

CHAPTER 7

144,000 are sealed [(7:1)]

Four messengers stand at the four corners of the earth to prevent the wind from blowing on the land or sea. Another messenger ascends from the orient, having the seal of the living God. He cries to the four, Do not injure the land or sea or trees until we seal the slaves of our God on their foreheads. The number of those sealed would be 144,000 out of every tribe of the sons of Israel; 12,000 of each of the 12 tribes.

There has been MUCH speculation as to the identity of these 144,000, with many liberties taken. Despite the fact that each of the 12 tribes of Israel are named, the most popular interpretation is that the 144,000 represents the church. But ...

> # What we see here is God securing the remnant of Israel in the midst of these judgments and persecutions taking place during the Great Tribulation.

In Matthew 24:31 we learn that after the Tribulation, angels are commissioned to gather the *elect* from the four winds. In His earthly ministry Jesus always addressed Israel; not the nations. So, we understand the *elect* to be Israel, and not the church.

As for the seal upon their heads, it is interesting that the Romans marked their soldiers on the hand, and their servants on the forehead.

As the tribes are named we see Levi and Joseph appearing in place of Dan and Ephraim. Remember they were blotted out for introducing idolatry into Israel. (Judges 18; 1 Kings 12:28-30; Deuteronomy 29:18-26) But they will be restored to their allotment in the land (Ezekiel 48) when the kingdom comes.

Meanwhile, in heaven ...

The multitude in white robes (7:9)

A vast throng out of every nation and tribe and people and language stand before the throne and before the Lambkin clothed in white robes and with palm fronds. They cry, Salvation be our God's Who is sitting on the throne, and the Lambkin's.

This vast throng comes OUT OF every nation but are Israelites. Jews are scattered among all the nations.

All the messengers and elders and animals around the throne fall down on their faces and worship.

One of the elders tells me the ones clothed in white robes are those coming out of the great affliction. They whiten their robes in the blood of the Lambkin. They are before the throne of God and offer divine service to Him day and night in His temple. He Who sits on the throne will be tabernacling over them. They will not hunger or thirst any longer, nor should the sun nor heat fall on them. The Lambkin will shepherd and guide them to living springs of water, and every tear will God brush away from their eyes.

CHAPTER 8

Seal #7: The golden censer (8:1)

Seal #7 is opened: A hush in heaven, as it were half an hour.

> Silence! A brief reprieve from the outpouring of calamities.

Seven trumpets are given to the seven messengers standing before God. Another messenger comes with a golden thurible. Incense is given to him to impart to the prayers of all the saints on the golden altar before the throne. The fumes of the incense ascend before God with the prayers of the saints.

> Incense is a picture of prayers ascending to God. (Psalm 141:2)

> The seven messengers could be the same as those given to pour out the seven bowls (15:1) and the seven spirits before the throne (1:4), one of whom is Gabriel (Luke 1:19). The seventh seal covers the entire period of judgment as seen in the trumpets and vials (8:7-18:24) and is immediately followed by the coming of the Son of Man in power and glory.

The messenger crams the thurible with fire from the altar and casts it into the earth. Thunders and voices and lightnings and an earthquake occur.

> These words are much like Ezekiel 10:5,8 where fire is taken from between the cherubim and cast over Jerusalem to prophesy its doom. The cherubim were always at the center of Israel's worship, and generally were a signal for judgment.

The trumpets (8:6)

Trumpet #1 sounds: Hail and fire mixed with blood are cast into the earth and a third of the earth is burned up. All green grass is burned up.

> 1/3 of the earth is burned.

> The trumpet judgments parallel the plagues in Egypt. The first plague was the turning of the waters into blood. (Exodus 7:14-25)

> Judgment is an interesting work of God. It is temporary, and it is intermediate (not a final condition). It is always with purpose. It is a part of the divine *process* and leads to God's ultimate purpose to become All in all.

Trumpet #2 sounds: A huge mountain burning with fire is cast into the sea. A third of the sea becomes blood, and a third of the sea creatures having a soul die. A third of the ships decay.

> 1/3 of the sea is destroyed.

Trumpet #3 sounds: A large star falls out of heaven, burning as a torch. It falls on a third of the rivers and springs of water. The name of the star is Absinth, and a third of the waters become absinth, and many of mankind die of the waters as they are made bitter.

> 1/3 of the waters are made bitter and unusable. Absinthin is the bitter principle component of wormwood, and is highly poisonous when taken in large doses.

Trumpet #4 sounds: A third of the sun and moon and stars are eclipsed and darkened. A vulture flies in mid-heaven saying, Woe to those dwelling on the earth as a result of the remaining three trumpets that will sound.

> 1/3 of the sun, moon, and stars are darkened.

CHAPTER 9

Trumpet #5 sounds: A star falls to the earth out of heaven. To him is given the key of the well of the submerged chaos.

> Angels are called stars in Job 38:7, and often in the Old Testament the phrase "host of heaven" refers to angels. (1 Kings 22:19; 2 Chronicles 18:18; Joshua 5:14.)

He opens the well, and fumes ascend as the smoke of a large furnace. The sun and air are darkened by the fumes, and out of the fumes there come locusts. License is given to these locusts as scorpions, but they are instructed not to injure the grass or tree or any green thing; but only those of mankind that do not have God's seal on their foreheads. They are not to kill, but torment for five months. Men will seek death but not find it. These locusts are like horses made ready for battle, with faces like humans and teeth like lions.

Many will speculate as to the identity of these monstrous locusts; making them man-made devices of war. But let us be content with God's description. They are creatures designed by God to accomplish His purposes. If they are figurative and representative of something, the explanation of that something is not provided by God. Rather than speculate, let us just note that great pain is experienced by those upon the earth not sealed by God.

A description of the locusts can be found in Joel 1:4 and 2:2-4. Common locusts destroy only vegetation (Exodus 10:5,12,15). But these locusts from the submerged chaos are designed for a different purpose, and human beings are their victims; not vegetation.

Observe that the length of this torment is five months. Duration of torment will vary. Torment accompanies disease (Matthew 4:24; 8:6) and is a form of physical distress. The disciples suffered from the torment of overexertion and worry. (Mark 6:48) For the wild beast and false prophet it will last for the eons of the eons. So, torment is suffered by various beings. It is never threatened as the penalty of sin, except for those hearing the eonian evangel (Revelation 14:6).

The sound of their wings is like many chariot horses racing into battle. They have tails like scorpions with which to injure mankind. Their king is the messenger of the submerged chaos; Abaddon in Hebrew and Apollyon in Greek.

The fallen star is often said to be Satan. But Satan is not the only instrument of evil used by God. In this vision Apollyon is the head of these scorpion-like locusts. His very name is *Destruction*, but he is not Satan. The fallen star is a messenger of God, appearing in obedience to the trumpet call.

So, the abyss is unlocked, and locusts that are like scorpions torture those not sealed by God. The term *abyss* is always associated with the waters of the earth. The springs of the abyss were broken up at the flood. (Genesis 7:11; 8:2) In Isaiah we read of the waters of the great deep, or abyss. (Isaiah 51:10)

In the opening of Joel's prophecy locusts represented the four Assyrian invasions that devastated the land.

Trumpet #6 sounds: The four messengers bound at the river Euphrates are loosed, having been made ready to kill a third of mankind. The cavalry numbers 200 million. The heads of the horses are like lions and their tails like serpents, and from their mouths issue fire and fumes and sulphur. A third of mankind are killed. The remainder of mankind not killed do not repent of their acts; worshipping demons and idols, murder, enchantments, prostitution, and theft.

> 1/3 of mankind is killed by these messengers. Despite the continuing calamities, man refuses to repent. From this we can infer that God's purpose in bringing these judgments is to cause repentance. At this point in the process, though, repentance has not yet come.
>
> The idols that are worshipped are not innocent inanimate objects. The religions of the nations are not of human origin. Paul observed that what the nations were sacrificing to were demons. (1 Corinthians 10:20) Paul tells us there are many gods (1 Corinthians 8:5) but for us there is only One. Behind the idols of gold and silver are unseen but powerful powers of darkness. The worship of these idols is, then, the worship of demons. It is a false religion.
>
> So, the sixth messenger sends forth four other messengers; apparently to eliminate Godless religions, including Christ-less christianity. Christianity is Christ-less, for long before those in Christ will have ascended into glory at the call of the Lord. But this "snatching away" (1 Thessalonians 4:13ff) is not the end of the Christian "church" which will continue in apostasy.
>
> We get a glimpse of the organization of these angels who act as messengers. Each has been given special jurisdiction. Four have control of the winds (7:1), Abaddon is the messenger of the Abyss (9:11), and there is a messenger of the waters (16:5).
>
> In the Old Testament trumpets were used to call people together (Numbers 10:1), to announce war (Numbers 10:9), and to announce special times (Numbers 10:10).

CHAPTER 10

The angel and the little scroll (10:1)

Another messenger descends out of heaven, holding a tiny open scroll. He cries with a loud voice, with his right foot on the sea and his left foot on the land. As he cries out the seven thunders speak, but I was told to seal that which the seven thunders spoke and not to record these things.

> Throughout Revelation, angels are the ministers of God's will. The descent of this messenger is the formal taking possession of the earth in the name of the King; though ACTUAL occupation of the throne takes place later in chapter 19.

> God instructs John as to how much of what he sees is to be revealed to mankind. Our curious nature wants to know all details about everything, but God is in control over what is revealed to us.

The messenger proclaims that there will be no further delay, and when the seventh messenger trumpets the secret of God is consummated.

I am told to get the tiny scroll and to devour it. It would make my bowels bitter but in my mouth it would be sweet as honey. I am told, You must prophesy again over peoples and nations and languages and many kings.

> Eating is a Hebrew idiom for receiving knowledge, as we would speak of digesting that which we have read or been taught.

CHAPTER 11

The two witnesses (11:1)

I was told to measure the temple of God and the altar and those worshiping in it; but not the court outside the temple for it was given to the nations, and they will be treading the holy city for 42 months.

> Where could we possibly see the Church, with these references to the temple, the altar, and the court of the Gentiles?

> In Ezekiel 40-41 and Zechariah 2:1-3 measurements were made to claim ownership. The outer court is omitted because it was left to be trodden by the nations until the coming of Christ.

> This 42-month period probably corresponds to the last half (3-1/2 years) of Daniel's 70th heptad. (Daniel 9:27) He tells of a prince that would come, making a treaty with the majority of the Jews, breaking the treaty after 3-1/2 years.

> The judgment had begun 3-1/2 years before and it will continue for another 3-1/2 years, but this center point is the high water mark for human apostasy. The covenant of Daniel 9:27 is made 3-1/2 years before,

but now in the middle of the heptad the covenant is broken and the persecution of Israel breaks out in a big way.

Two witnesses will prophesy 1260 days clothed in sackcloth. They are the two olive trees and the two lampstands which stand before the Lord of the earth. If anyone wants to injure them they must be killed. Fire will issue from their mouth and devour their enemies.

> God has never left Himself without witnesses among mankind. As for the identity of these two witnesses there is much speculation. But their identity does not matter, even if evidence can be gathered in support of a theory. As E. W. Bullinger asks, "Why cannot we leave them alone? If God wished us to know He could have told us."

They have authority to lock heaven that there may be no rain for the days of their prophecy. They have authority to turn the waters to blood, and to smite the land with every calamity.

> Elijah was once given authority to withhold rain. (James 5:17) Some contend that the two witnesses are Moses and Elijah, but this is simply speculation. But certainly they are in the spirit and power of Moses and Elijah.
>
> It is interesting to consider that God could wipe all evil from the earth in an instant. He could destroy the wild beast the instant he appeared. But He chooses not to eradicate evil, as it apparently serves a purpose in reaching the hearts of men.

When they finish their testimony the wild beast that ascended from the submerged chaos will conquer and kill them, and their corpses will be at the square of the great city, spiritually being called Sodom and Egypt, where their Lord was crucified. Those out of the peoples and tribes and languages and nations will observe their corpses 3 ½ days, not allowing them to be placed in tombs. Those dwelling on the earth will rejoice, sending presents to one another, seeing that these two prophets tormented those dwelling on the earth.

> Psalm 79 speaks of these *dead bodies of thy servants* and that *there were none to bury them.* All of Psalm 79, and additionally Psalms 9 and 10 can be read with an association to this episode in Revelation.

> The witnesses cannot be killed until their testimony is finished. Only then will God allow their deaths. But even their deaths and subsequent resurrection will be a witness to the world ...

After 3 ½ days the spirit of life out of God will enter into them and they will stand on their feet. Great fear will fall upon those beholding this, and they will hear a loud voice out of heaven saying, Ascend here. They will ascend into heaven in a cloud as their enemies observe. In that hour a great earthquake will occur, and a tenth of the city will fall. 7000 men will be killed in the earthquake, and the rest will be frightened and give glory to the God of heaven.

The seventh trumpet (11:15)

Trumpet #7 sounds: Loud voices in heaven say, The kingdom of this world became our Lord's and His Christ's, and He shall be reigning *for the eons of the eons.*

> The seventh trumpet is the crisis of human history. Man's day is ending. The sovereignty over the earth passes from man, the instrument of Satan, to the Son of Man. This seventh trumpet will later be expanded into the seven bowls in chapter 16. It takes in all of the remaining judgments and visions in heaven and on earth. This occupies about half of the book of Revelation.

> This seventh trumpet is not *the last trump* that we see in 1 Thessalonians 4:13ff. It is but the last in this *series* of seven trumpets.

> The sounding of this trumpet produces a great stir in heaven. It is the proclamation of the coming coronation of the rightful king of earth. (See also 2 Samuel 15:10 and 1 Kings 1:39.)

> # He will reign for the eons of the eons!

> He will not reign *forever and ever* for we are told Christ will reign UNTIL all is subjected to Him (1 Corinthians 15:25), at which point He will subject Himself to God the Father and cease reigning. He will reign *for*

the eons of the eons; at least two eons (periods of time) out of all of the eons.

The 24 elders fall on their faces and worship God, thanking the Lord God Almighty Who is and Who was, for He has taken His great power and reigns.

> Now, instead of being the Lord Who is, was and shall be; God is now described as the Lord Who is and was; for the "shall be" has now come. That which was always spoken of as future has now arrived, as John observes the beginning of the reign upon the earth.

> This "temple section" of Revelation represents the same events as described previously from the earth's perspective. We also see this when comparing the books of Kings and Chronicles; the same events but from two perspectives; Kings from the human perspective and Chronicles from the divine.

The nations are angered. His indignation has come, and the era for the judging of the dead, and for the giving of wages to His slaves, prophets, saints, and those fearing His name; and to blight those who are blighting the earth.

The temple of God in heaven is opened, and in it is the ark of God's covenant. Lightnings and voices and thunders and an earthquake and great hail occur.

> Again, this "temple section" covers the same era as the previous section. Both end with the establishing of Christ's kingdom, both share information on the 144,000 (7:4 and 14:1) and the wild beast (11:7; 13:1). But now these things are considered from a different perspective. The previous section began with a vision of the throne, signifying political dominion. This section begins with a vision of the temple, signifying worship. It is now the era of world-wide worship of God, and the world must be rid of false religions and philosophies.

> The seventh trumpet is sounded by a messenger. When the Lord comes for those in Christ (1 Thessalonians 4:16) He will descend from heaven with the shout of command and with the trumpet of God. This trumpet will be sounded by THE messenger, the Lord Himself, and not another. He is the Chief Messenger, and only His voice can wake the dead. He will be trumpeting. (1 Corinthians 15:52)

Why is this called *the last trump?*

This cannot be taken absolutely, but only relatively. Every time a trumpet is blown there is a "last trump" or final blast. Even the seventh trumpet which ushers in the kingdom here in Revelation is not the last time a trumpet will sound. In the temple ritual and festivals the redeemed earth will again hear the trumpet. The seventh is the last in the *series* sounded here.

Furthermore, nothing we read here in association with the seventh trumpet is consistent with what we see at the last trump in 1 Thessalonians 4. The kingdom ushered in by the seventh trumpet is the sovereignty of Israel over the nations. The nations are angered. (11:18) The Body of Christ has no place in this! Furthermore, at this seventh blast the Lord does not descend to the earth, the kingdom is not setup, and no judgment of the nations follows. No dead are raised, no living ones are changed from a terrestrial body to a celestial one. Instead, with the seventh trumpet many are killed, not raised. Israel's resurrection does not take place until 45 days after the seventh trumpet sounds.

The Thessalonians were sorrowing for their dead. What consolation could be found for those of the nations in connection with the seventh trumpet we read of here in Revelation? The nations are angry. Only Israel receives reward for faithful work.

The seven trumpets deal with the nations, or gentiles who have taken political possession of the earth; not the Body of Christ.

CHAPTER 12

The woman and the dragon (12:1)

A great *sign* is seen in heaven; a woman clothed with the sun, with the moon under her feet, and a wreath of twelve stars on her head. She is pregnant and is crying, travailing and tormented to be bringing forth.

This being a "sign" it must be taken figuratively; not literally.

Think back to Genesis 37 which is the only scripture corresponding to this sign. In Genesis, Joseph tells of his dream of the sun and moon and eleven stars that bowed down to him. Now the same twelve stars are seen in Revelation, this time with Joseph being the twelfth.

In most of the judgment scenes the beast is on the earth, and it is against him that the plagues of the Seals and Trumpets are directed.

There is another *sign* in heaven; a great fiery dragon with seven heads and ten horns and with diadems on each head. Its tail drags a third of the stars from heaven and casts them to the earth. The dragon stands before the woman waiting to devour her child when she brings it forth.

Defection in the heavens! A third of the angels cast their lot with the Adversary. The seven heads and ten horns portray the great confederacy, led by Satan, that will control the earth in the end times.

Where is Satan?

Satan is generally thought to preside in "hell." But until the end times he has access to heaven and earth, as in the days of Job. As a dragon he is in heaven, and then comes to the earth. Later we find him back in heaven, battling with Michael. Michael and his messengers eject him from the heavens. Later still he is chained in the abyss for 1000 years (20:12) before reappearing on the earth briefly. (20:7-9) Then he is cast into the lake of fire for the eons. (20:10)

Satan once used Herod in attempting to kill the child Jesus. Satan's objective was once to destroy the entire male line, making the birth of the seed of the woman impossible. Jehoram slew all his brethren so the royal line was reduced to one; him (2 Chronicles 21:4). But he had children, and Ahaziah was later the only lineal descendent of the royal line. She had children, but all were killed by Athaliah; except one that escaped his fate. And in the book of Esther an attempt was made to destroy the entire nation. Now, in Revelation, Satan will try once again to destroy Israel.

Today the dragon is the true ruler of the nations. The dragon is the antithesis of the gentle and harmless lambkin. It is a picture of evil; representing Satan's character and activities in the end times.

When confronting Eve in the Garden of Eden, Satan did not appear as a dragon. He did not wish to cause fear; but confidence. Satan sometimes appears as an angel of light (2 Corinthians 11:14), but at other times he is as a roaring lion (1 Peter 5:8). He changes in appearance to suit the occasion. Here he assumes the role of a dragon, leaving behind the disguise of a deceiver to become the ferocious adversary.

The woman brings forth a son who will shepherd all the nations with an iron club. The child is snatched away to God and to His throne. The woman flees into the wilderness, to a place made ready by God, for her to be nourished for 1260 days.

Our Lord foretold this flight of the woman (Matthew 24:15-22; Mark 13:14-20). All in Judea are warned to flee to the mountains with great haste. And so the woman flees into the wilderness where she is sustained in a supernatural manner.

Remember the woman is a "sign" and not literally a woman. She appears to represent Israel. This "male son" is probably the 144,000; the conquerors. Those who emerge from Israel during her time of trial will be God's representatives among the nations. Israel will be under the authority of the twelve apostles; but the outside world will be ruled by the 144,000. The millennial reign will not be a system of mutual agreements between nations. It will be a despotism. The law will go forth from Jerusalem and it will be enforced among all nations with an iron club.

A battle takes place in heaven. Michael and his messengers battle with the dragon and its messengers. But they are not strong enough, nor was their place still found in heaven.

Michael is always associated with Israel. In Daniel's last vision he is described as *the great chief who stands for the sons of your people* (Daniel 12:1). This Daniel passage concords very closely with this present description in Revelation, where Michael stands up and casts down to earth the Slanderer.

The great dragon is cast out; the ancient serpent called Adversary and Satan who is deceiving the whole inhabited earth. It is cast into the earth along with its messengers. A loud voice in heaven says, Just now came the salvation and the power and the kingdom of our God, and the authority of His Christ, for the accuser of our brethren was cast out, who was accusing them before our God day and night. They conquer him through the blood of the Lambkin and through the word of their testimony, and they love not their soul until death. Make merry ye heavens and those tabernacaling in them. Woe to the land and sea, for the Adversary descended to you having great fury, being aware that his season is brief.

> This vision tells us the result upon the earth of the war in heaven. First we are told of the effect concerning Israel; and then as it effects the entire earth.
>
> Jesus saw Satan fall in Luke 10:18. We also see this foretold in Isaiah 14:12-15. When the dragon attacks Jerusalem it comes into conflict with Michael, one of the chief princes (Daniel 10:13). Michael is Israel's prince (Daniel 10:21) in God's "government." Michael and his messengers eject the dragon and its messengers out of heaven.
>
> So, presently Satan is in heaven (Job 1:6; Ephesians 6:12) and will not be ejected until the middle of Daniel's 70th week.

When the dragon sees it is cast to the earth, it persecutes the woman who brought forth the son. The woman is given two wings as a large vulture, that she may fly into the wilderness to the place made ready where she will be nourished a season, and seasons, and half a season, from the serpent's face.

> Clearly the woman is Israel which brought forth the child (Christ). She will be nourished for 3 $\frac{1}{2}$ years; the second half of the 7-year period of tribulation.
>
> Compare these events with Matthew 24:16 when the Lord counsels faithful Israel to flee into the mountains of Judea (a wilderness) when they see the abomination of desolation (Daniel 9:27) standing in the holy place. This tells us these events are in the middle of the last heptad.

The serpent casts water like a river out of its mouth to carry the woman away by its current. The earth helps the woman, opening its mouth and swallowing the river. The dragon is angry with the woman and comes away to do battle with the rest of her seed who are keeping the precepts of God and who have the testimony of Jesus.

The Body of Christ has previously been snatched up to be with Christ (1 Thessalonians 4:13ff). Satan's goal seems to be in sight upon the earth. Unable to destroy the child, he turns his attention to the remainder of Israel.

Consider Daniel 7-12

Before we proceed further, let us consider the final six chapters of Daniel. There are many similarities, and a consideration of this Old Testament prophecy will provide some valuable background. To put this into context, Daniel lived from 605-530 BC, and he wrote his account while exiled in Babylonia after the defeat of Judah.

Daniel's first vision (Daniel 7:1)

I was perceiving in my vision during the night. Four monstrous animals were coming up from the sea. The eastern animal was like a lioness, and she had the wings of a vulture. Her wings were scraped smooth. She was made to stand on two feet like a mortal. (7:2)

> The lioness from the east with vulture's wings that were scraped smooth, requiring the creature to move on its feet, could represent Buddhism. Centered in East Asia, Buddhism once used its wings to leave India and spread to the Himalayas, Kashmir, Tibet, Nepal, China, Japan, Burma, Siam, and Ceylon. But with its wings scraped smooth it has lost the power to spread and has remained within its confines ever since.

Another animal, like a she-bear. They were saying to her, rise! Devour huge amounts of flesh. (7:5)

> The she-bear could represent Hinduism, centered in India.

Another animal, like a leopardess, had four wings and four heads, and jurisdiction was granted to her. (7:6)

> The leopardess could represent the Arab world. Its wings could picture the swift spread of Islam.

A fourth animal, terrifying and dreadful and exceedingly mighty. She had monstrous iron teeth, and she was devouring and crushing and stamping upon the remainder with her feet. She was diverse from all the animals that were east of her, and she had ten horns. (7:7)

> With the other animals located east of her, this monstrous creature is based in the west. This could represent Christendom, based in Europe and America. It is not that *Christianity* is this beast. But when, under Constantine, authority was given to it, Christianity became *Christendom*, the fourth beast. Christendom is not those who are the Body of Christ. But *organized* Christianity as a "*religion*" has become Christendom, and is perhaps represented by this fourth beast. Remember that the Body of Christ; Christianity; has been removed from the scene before the events described in Revelation; having been "snatched-away" per 1 Thessalonians 4:13ff.

> While nations and political powers rise and fall, these four religion-groups have remained constant. And we will see the four become united under the leadership of the dragon in Revelation 12. As for the ten horns of this fourth beast, while nations have come and gone there can typically be ten identified at any given time that comprise the western nations of Christendom. These ten are those nations in the picture in The Day of the Lord.

> In Daniel the four beasts are distinct from one another, as are the world religions today (for the most part). But in Revelation we will see them merged into one. Observe that the fourth beast does not completely destroy the other three, for they remain when the fourth beast is destroyed.

Another bit of horn came up among them, and three of the eastern horns were uprooted. There were eyes like the eyes of a mortal in this horn, and a mouth declaring monstrous things, and it was making war with the saints. (7:8)

> While the other horns represent political-religious powers, this little horn with eyes and a mouth would seem to be a personality; not just a power.

I was perceiving until thrones were situated, and the Transferror of Days sat down. The scrolls were opened. (7:9)

The animal was despatched. As for the remainder of the animals, their authority was caused to pass away; yet a lengthening of life was granted to them until the stated time and season. (7:11)

These three kingdoms, then, did not go away. Their duration is prolonged even after their jurisdiction (authority) passes from them. They are still religious organizations. They are called kingdoms because they usurp the functions that belong to the sphere of government. This seems a bit foreign to us today, for there is a separation (for the most part) between politics and religion. But considering what Christendom became in the decades following Constantine's decree, and considering the strong alliance between the Arab nations and Islam, it is easy to understand how the beasts, which might seem to represent political powers, are really religious powers.

With the clouds of the heavens One like a son of a mortal was arriving. To Him was granted jurisdiction and esteem and a kingdom, that all the peoples and leagues and language-groups shall serve Him. His jurisdiction is an eonian jurisdiction that shall not pass away, and His kingdom shall not be confined. (7:13)

It is not that this jurisdiction will <u>never</u> pass away, for there will come a time when God becomes All in all, and no authority or jurisdiction is needed. But this *eonian jurisdiction* will not be conquered or pass away *for the eons.*

These four monstrous animals are four kingdoms that shall arise from the earth. Yet the saints of the supremacies shall receive the kingdom, and they shall safeguard the kingdom unto the eon, even unto the eon of the eons. (7:17)

As for the fourth animal, the horn was making an attack on the saints and was prevailing against them, until the Transferror of Days arrived, and adjudication was granted to the saints, and *the stated time came* when the saints safeguarded the kingdom. (7:21)

These beasts will have their day, but only until *the stated time* comes; at which time the Lord ("The Transferrer of Days") arrives to establish His kingdom.

As for the fourth animal, there shall come to be a fourth kingdom on the earth that is diverse from all the other kingdoms. She shall devour the entire earth and thresh it and crush it. As for the ten horns, from this kingdom shall ten kings arise; and another one shall arise after them. He shall abase three kings. Declarations against the Supreme shall he declare, and to the saints of the supremacies shall he bring decay. They shall be granted into his hand for a season and two seasons and half a season. Then adjudication shall be seated, and they shall cause his authority to pass away, so as to exterminate and to destroy him until the terminus. (7:23)

> Again, at the stated time when the Lord arrives ("The Adjudicator"), the authority of the beasts shall be taken from them.
>
> Who are these beasts? They embrace the entire earth. This should prevent us from assigning them with any nation in existence today.
>
> Religion is the distinguishing characteristic of these beasts; not politics. We see here a confederation of false religions that seek to destroy the only religion that is of God. We should not seek to match today's *nations* with the beasts described in Daniel or in Revelation. Instead we look at *religions*, for the wild beast of Revelation (which is a combination of the four beasts in Daniel) is primarily a religious empire.
>
> So, while many interpreters see these creatures and the ten horns as nations comprising a revived Roman empire; it seems more likely that the creatures represent world religions; with the ten horns being nations under the dominant religion in the end times.

And the kingdom and the jurisdiction and the majesty of the kingdom under the entire heavens will be granted to the people of the saints of the supremacies. Their kingdom is an eonian kingdom, and all other authorities shall serve and hearken to them. (7:27)

Daniel's second vision (Daniel 8:1)

I saw a ram with two horns, one loftier than the other. The loftier one was coming up last. I saw the ram rushing forth westward, northward and southward. No animals could stand before him, and there was no rescuing from his hand. (8:3)

As I was considering this, a he-goat was coming from the west over the surface of the entire earth, without touching the earth. It had a conspicuous horn between his eyes, and he came unto the ram. He smote the ram and broke his two horns. He flung the ram to the earth and tramped him down, and no one came to the rescue of the ram. (8:5)

The he-goat grew exceedingly great, but as soon as he became staunch the great horn was broken, and in its stead came up four other conspicuous horns toward the four winds of the heavens. Then from one of them a single inferior horn came forth, and grew excelling great to the southland and to the sunrise and to the stately land. He grew great unto the host of the heavens. (8:8)

And there was cast to the earth some from the host, and one from the stars, who tramped them down. Even unto the chief of the host he arrogated greatness to himself. Because of him the continuous ritual was disturbed, and the furnishing of His sanctuary was flung down. And the horn was given a host for transgression against the continuous ritual. Thus he acted and prospered. (8:10)

For how long is the vision of the continuous ritual; the cessation of the sacrifice and the desolating transgression where the holy place and the host are tramped down? Unto 2,300 evening-mornings. Then the holy place will come into its right. (8:13)

> # Now comes the explanation provided to Daniel.

A voice said to Gabriel, make this one understand the sight. And he said to me, understand, son of humanity, that the vision is for the era of the end. I am acquainting you with what is coming in the last of the menace to the sons of your people, seeing that it is for the appointed time of the end. (8:15)

The ram having two horns is the kingdom of Media and Persia. The he-goat is the kingdom of Greece. The great horn is the first king. When it is broken, four kingdoms from his nation shall stand up, yet not with his vigor. (8:20)

> I will cite some historical references that would seem to be the fulfillments (at least partial fulfillments) of events described in Daniel and Revelation. But remember that various sources differ in their opinions regarding these events. Those cited seem to be the most plausible in my mind, but keep in mind that *none* of these historical events represents the *total* fulfillment which shall only be seen in the end times; days we have not yet seen.

The Medo-Persian empire seems to have been centered at Shushan, southwest of Babylon. While the Medes were more powerful from the military perspective, they seem to have been conquered by Persia by treachery. And as the strength of this second horn grew, it moved westward; conquering Babylonia, Lydia, Greece, Armenia, Scythia, Ethiopia, Egypt, and Lybia; thereby becoming a world empire.

Clearly this speaks of Alexander the Great, whose reign was dominant, but short (13 years). At his premature death at age 32 the kingdom he had built was divided into four parts:

Lysimachus: Thrace and Bithynia.
Cassander: Macedonia and Greece.
Seleucus: Syria, Babylonia, east to India.
Ptolomy: Egypt, Palestine, Arabia, Petrea.

All of this is in the past. But now we move to the future ...

And IN THE LATTER TIME of their kingdom there shall stand up a king of strong presence and understanding problems. His vigor will be staunch, yet not by his own vigor. Marvelously shall he ruin, and he will prosper and deal. Thus he ruins the staunch and the people of the saints. By his intelligence he causes deceit to prosper. In his heart he shall arrogate greatness to himself, and while they are at ease he shall ruin many. Against the Chief of chiefs shall he stand, yet at the limit of his hand he shall be broken. (8:23)

So, we move from the past (Alexander and then his four successors) to "the latter time" in the future. Josephus finds fulfillment in the exploits of Antiochus Epiphanes, some 408 years after Daniel's prophecy. Antiochus was determined to unify his kingdom both religiously and socially, and he led a brutal suppression of Jewish worship. In 168 BC he seized Jerusalem on the Sabbath, erected an idol of Zeus, and desecrated the altar by offering a swine on it. This became known to the Jews as the abomination of desolation.

Antiochus died in 164 BC, and a year later Judas Maccabaeus rededicated the Jerusalem temple and re-started the daily sacrifices; 3 years and 55 days after Antiochus had abolished all sacrifices. Today this is celebrated as Hanukkah.

> # But the words of Jesus show that all of this was not the fulfillment of Daniel's prophecy.

Let me repeat ... the words of Jesus show that these historic events WERE NOT THE FULFILLMENT of Daniel's prophecy, for he speaks of the abomination of desolation declared by Daniel as a FUTURE event (Matthew 24:15). Antiochus Epiphanes was just a shadow of that which is to come.

It is not uncommon for prophecy to find a partial fulfillment in the short term, and an ultimate fulfillment later. An example would be the virgin who was to give birth to a child (Isaiah 7:14 and Matthew 1:23); fulfilled in Old Testament times but ultimately fulfilled by Christ. We know there was a short-term fulfillment, for Isaiah was providing a *sign* to Ahaz. This would not have been a *sign to Ahaz* had a virgin not given birth in that day. Still, the short-term fulfillment was only partial. The ultimate fulfillment arrived with the birth of Christ.

THE SEVENTY SEVENS (Daniel 9:21)

Gabriel came saying, Daniel, I have come forth now to give you insight and understanding. (9:21)

Seventy sevens are segregated for your people and for your holy city; to detain transgression, to make sin come to end, to make a propitiatory shelter for depravity, to bring the righteousness of the eons, to seal the vision and the prophetic word, to anoint the holy of holies. (9:24)

"For your people" shows us this speaks to the Jews, Daniel's people.

From the going forth of the word to cause a return and to rebuild Jerusalem; from then until Messiah the Governor is 7-sevens and 62-sevens. After the 62-sevens, Messiah shall be cut off, and there will be no adjudication for Him. The city and the holy place shall be laid in ruins, with the other governor's coming. (9:25)

The events of this prophecy commence with the decree to rebuild Jerusalem. The rebuilding takes place after the initial 7-sevens (49 years). After another 62-sevens (434 years) Messiah comes, but He is "cut off" (crucified). A pause takes place due to Israel's rebellion, leading to Paul's commissioning to gather the Body of Christ. The final "seven" (7 years) continues to await fulfillment. But the hardening of Israel will come to an end (Romans 11:25) once God has fulfilled His purposes, after which the Body of Christ will be removed from the scene to fulfill its destiny in the heavens (1 Thessalonians 4), and the final 7-year period as described in Revelation will take place.

The secrets of the Kingdom (Matthew 13) were revealed only after the heralding of the Kingdom's nearness had been rejected.

> # This rejection of the kingdom and the king was not seen by Daniel, and accounts for a lengthening of time (or a pause) between the 69th seven and the final seven.

He will be master of a covenant with many for 1-seven. At half of the 7 he shall cause to cease the sacrifice and the approach present. On a wing of the sanctuary shall be desolating abominations. (9:27)

So, the final 7-year period is divided in half. A covenant to allow the restoration of Israel's temple worship is interrupted at the 3 1/2-year mark; unleashing the severe persecution and calamities in the final 3 1/2 years prior to the Lord's return.

Gabriel delayed in coming (Daniel 10:1)

I saw a great sight, yet those with me did not see the sight. He said to me, understand the words that I am speaking to you, for I have been sent to you. (10:7)

Yet the chief of the kingdom of Persia was standing to confront me twenty-one days. But Michael, one of the first chiefs, came to help me. And I left him there beside the chief of the kings of Persia. (10:13)

He said to me, I have come to make you understand what shall befall your people in the latter days; for the vision is for future days. Then I shall return to fight with the chief of the kingdom of Persia. (10:14)

"What shall befall YOUR people." All of this is centered on Israel; Daniel's people.

That which we see in the natural world is controlled by unseen, external, irresistible forces. It is these spiritual forces that organize man into religious bodies that become powerful, and that in the end times seems to succeed in driving God out of the earth. That appears to be Satan's objective once he is cast from the heavens; to consume the entire earth and to drive God completely from that realm. Today men are at the mercy of spiritual powers, and much that occurs in the world is attributed to this unseen realm. *We wrestle not with blood and flesh but with the spiritual forces of wickedness among the celestials.* (Ephesians 6:12) If we could see beyond those who seemingly attack us we would find the spirit realm working thru them.

Men might think religion is a means to worship God; an organized way to glorify God upon the earth. Those within Islam are certain they have the true faith and that all others are infidels. Christendom possesses an outward shell of truth and a form of godliness based on God's Word, but is lacking life and power.

It could be out of Christendom that the large horn will arise that speaks monstrous things to set aside God.

Remember, true Christianity; the Body of Christ; has been removed from the scene before the events of Revelation.

For many years there have been movements to combine the best in all religions for the sake of good. These movements would seem to be a precursor to the ultimate combining of the four beasts (world religions) into a single monstrous beast in the end times.

Power struggles between nations [(Daniel 11:1)]

Three kings will yet stand up in Persia. The fourth shall be enriched with riches greater than all. He shall rouse the whole kingdom of Greece. Then stands up a master king. (11:2)

> Following Cyrus came four Medo-Persian kings; Cambyses (530-522 BC), Gaumata (522 BC), Darius I Hystaspes (521-486 BC), and Xerxes (486-465 BC). The last was very rich and powerful, and is referred to as King Ahasuerus in the Book of Esther. When he gains power by wealth he stirs up the kingdom of Greece, but his army is defeated. The master king that rises is Alexander the Great.

While he stands his kingdom shall be broken up and divided to the four winds of the heavens, yet not to posterity. It will not be as his rule with which he ruled; for his kingdom shall be plucked up and given to others aside from these. (11:4)

> Alexander's kingdom did not go to his descendants. His son was assassinated and he had no living descendants. Instead the kingdom was divided between Cassander (Macedonia and Greece), Lyssmachus (Thrace and parts of Asia Minor), Ptolemy (Egypt and Palestine), and Seleucus (northern Syria and Mesopotamia).

Steadfast shall be a king of the southland. His daughter shall come to the king of the north to make equitable settlements, yet she shall not retain the vigor of the seed and will be given up. Yet one stands from the scion of her roots, and he shall lead the army. He shall enter into the stronghold of the king of the north. He will deal with him and be steadfast. Coveted furnishings of silver and gold shall he bring to Egypt in captivity. For some years he shall stand over the king of the north; when he comes into the kingdom of the king of the southland he will return to his ground. (11:5)

> In Egypt, Ptolemy (king of the south) became strong, but one of his commanders became stronger. This was Seleucus, in Syria and Mesopotamia. The daughter (Berenice) of the king of the south (Ptolemy II Philadelphia) goes to the king of the north (Antiochus II Theos of Syria) to make an alliance. They marry, but then Antiochus, Berenice, and her son are assassinated.

> Berenice's brother (Ptolemy III Euergetes) succeeds as king of Egypt. To avenge Berenice he invades Syria and overcomes Seleucus II.

> ## As with Antiochus, my belief is that these fulfillments were partial, and a shadow of the ultimate fulfillment in end times.

All of this depicts attempts that will be made to restore Alexander's empire in the end times. Many interpreters look for Rome to be at the center of events; a revival of the Roman empire. But nothing in the Scriptures speaks of Rome. Scripture seems to speak of Alexander's kingdom, divided and restored, and ultimately with supernatural assistance from the dragon.

His sons shall be stirred up, and they will gather a throng of many armies which will come to enter the southland, overwhelm it and pass on. Yet it shall return and be stirred up onto its strength. (11:10)

> Seleucus II began an attempt to invade Egypt in 242 BC. But this was a disaster and he returned with a remnant of his army. His son (Antiochus III the Great) assembled a great army and battled as far as his fortress.

Then the king of the southland shall be bitterly enraged and will march forth, and he will fight with the king of the north. He will recruit a vast throng. His heart will be high when he casts down tens of thousands, yet he shall not be strengthened. (11:11)

> Ptolemy IV of Egypt defeated Antiochus III in the Battle of Raphia in 217 BC. But he failed to follow up on this victory.

Then the king of the north will return and recruit a throng vaster than the former. Many shall stand against the king of the southland. The king of the north shall construct an earthwork, and will seize city fortresses. The armed forces of the king of the southland shall not stand nor his chosen people, for there will be no vigor to stand. (11:13)

> Insurrections broke out in Egypt after the death of Ptolemy IV when Ptolemy V was a child. Some Jews sided with Antiochus, but an anti-Egyptian revolt was subdued.

He who is coming against it shall do as is acceptable to himself, and there will be no one standing before him. Thus he shall stand in the stately land which will be entirely in his hand. Then he shall set his face to come with the might of all his kingdom, and equitable settlements. He will seize many places. (11:16)

> Antiochus III conquered Palestine in 198 BC. Taking advantage of Egypt's weakness he defeated Ptolemy V. Antiochus then attempted to conquer Asia Minor and Greece but was defeated at Magnesia in 190 BC.

Then he shall turn back his face to the strongholds of his own land. Yet he will stumble and fall and shall not be found. (11:19)

> Returning from Magnesia he plundered a temple at Elymais but was attacked by the people and killed in 187 BC.

Then there will stand out of his root a royal sprout. Yet he shall be broken, not in anger and not in battle. (11:20)

> Seleucus was assassinated in 175 BC.

> It seems likely that in the end times the focus will be on the king of the south, Egypt, when there is a definite king of the north. Then, it would seem, we can expect the opening scene of these end times to begin.

Then there will stand a despised person. Hence they do not bestow on him the splendor of the kingdom. Yet he will enter with ease and make steadfast the kingdom by slick dealings. He shall practice deceit. He shall come and do what his fathers had never done. Plunder and loot and goods he shall lavish on them, and against Egypt he shall devise his devices, yet only for a season. (11:21)

> To become king, Antiochus IV Epiphanes pushed aside Seleuceus' son Demetrius, who should have succeeded the throne. The high priest Onias III was assassinated in 171 BC. Antiochus led an expedition against Egypt in 170 BC and was successful.

In the end times, when this diplomat takes the position of king of the north, he will be so despised that he will not be given the usual honor as befits a king. His initial appearance will be in peace. He seems to have nothing behind him except brains and money. He must deal with the political currents that threaten to destroy him. He will be the premier diplomat, employing sly dealings.

He shall rouse his vigor and his heart against the king of the southland with his great army. And the king of the southland shall be stirred up for battle with his great and exceedingly staunch army, yet he shall not stand. (11:25)

Ptolemy Philometer was defeated at Mount Casius in a great slaughter.

Then the two kings, with evil in their hearts, will sit at one table. When he returns to his land with a great amount of goods, his heart will be on the holy covenant, and he will make it effective before he returns to his land. (11:27)

The two kings were Antiochus and Ptolemy Philometer. After his Egyptian campaign, Antiochus began his campaign to destroy Judaism.

In the end times, by making a holy covenant, he will gain the allegiance of a majority of Israel.

At the appointed time he shall return and come into the southland. Boats of Kittim will come against him, and he will be sore when he returns. He will menace the holy covenant and makes this effective. When he returns he shall have an understanding with those who forsake the holy covenant. His armed forces shall stand about. They will profane the sanctuary, the stronghold, take away the continuous ritual, and set up the abomination of desolation. Yet the people knowing their Elohim shall be steadfast and act accordingly. (11:29)

Antiochus Epiphanes tried to overtake the Egyptian empire but was warned by Rome that if he continued he would find himself at war with Rome. Remembering how his father was defeated by the Roman army at Magnesia, he ceased his attack and vented his anger on Jerusalem. Storming Jerusalem he massacred 80,000 men, women and children. Jerusalem was conquered in 168 BC and Antiochus decreed the Jewish religion to be forbidden. (These events were a shadow of the end times.)

> In the end times, he will begin by invoking the holy covenant and using it to gain the support of Israel. But when, in his defeat, he is offered universal dominion and headship of all religions, he will no longer uphold his edict and will turn against the holy covenant. Keep in mind that among the Jews there are many that are not "orthodox" and who have no sympathy with a return to the law or ritual. Besides, he has a military force to enforce his desires and plans.

The intelligent of the people shall cause many to understand, yet they are caused to stumble by the sword and the blaze, by captivity and plunder for days. (11:33)

The king does as is acceptable to himself. He shall exalt and magnify himself over every el [god]. Concerning the Elohim of his fathers he shall not understand. (11:36)

> This king, it seems, is an Israelite; with this reference to the Elohim of *his fathers.*

Then, in the era of the end, the king of the southland shall gore him, and the king of the north shall come against him like a hurricane. When he comes into the stately land, many shall stumble. He will rule by reserves of gold and silver. Yet reports shall fluster him, from the sunrise and from the north, and he will march forth with great fury to exterminate and to doom many. When he comes unto his end, there will be no help for him. (11:40)

> Antiochus (king of the north) overwhelmed Ptolemy (king of the south) and gained control of Libya and Ethiopia. Antiochus died in Persia.
>
> In the end times the king of the north will have been defeated earlier (11:29,30) but he now appears to be empowered by dark spiritual powers. He comes like a hurricane and sweeps away all opposition. His foe seems to be entrenched in Palestine, so he gathers the kings of the earth and their armies at Armageddon to wipe out the last remnant of divine worship that remains upon the earth. (Revelation 16:16; 19:19-21)
>
> There have been attempts to assign many specifics to the kings of Egypt, Syria, and elsewhere. Beyond the basic historic accounts we have provided, which seem the most plausible of those recorded, we will not attempt to go further.

While there may be historic fulfillments of these north-south power struggles, they are only *partial* fulfillments as was the case with Antiochus Epiphanes (which events the Lord would later say were still to come).

> # History has not yet seen fulfillment of the passage that follows.

In that era Michael shall stand up, the great chief who is standing over the sons of your people. Then an era of distress will come to pass such as has not occurred since there was a nation on the earth. In that era your people shall escape; all those found written in the scroll. From those sleeping in the soil of the ground many shall awake, these to eonian life and these to reproach for eonian repulsion. (12:1)

> Here, then, is the deliverance of Israel; a deliverance that occupies an entire era. The coming of Christ is not mentioned here as it is in Revelation.
>
> "Those written in the scroll" is another clear indication that Israel is the subject here. Israelites were accustomed to scrolls with lists of names. Their genealogies were among their most precious possessions. Paul, when he wishes to distinguish his helpers of the Circumcision from the others speaks of them as those whose names are in the scroll of life. (Philippians 4:3)

It is for an appointed time, two appointed times and half an appointed time. (12:7)

Go Daniel, for the words are stopped up and sealed until the era of the end. (12:9)

> Observe that it is not these visions recorded by Daniel that were to be stopped up and sealed, for they found their way into the Scriptures. It was the ACTION described in the visions that was stopped up until the appropriate time.

From the era when the continuous ritual is taken away, and to the setting of the abomination of desolation, is 1290 days. Happy is he who will tarry and attain to the 1335 days. (12:11)

> The 3-½ years as mentioned throughout (the last half of the final seven) would be 1260 days. Here we see 1290 days. Perhaps the additional 30 day period is needed for the priesthood to make the necessary arrangements to restore the true worship of God. And the additional 45 days (bringing the total to 1335 mentioned here) could be for the benefit of Daniel and others who had died and who awaited the resurrection ("the former resurrection"). Once all is ready within the kingdom it would be time for their rousing.

Now let us return to our study of Revelation.

Enter … the beast.

CHAPTER 13

The beast comes out of the sea (13:1)

As the dragon stands by the sea a wild beast ascends out of the sea, having ten horns and seven heads, with diadems and blasphemous names on its heads. The beast was like a leopardess, with feet like a bear and a mouth like a lion. The dragon gives the beast its power and throne and great authority.

> When the Dragon is cast down to earth it immediately proceeds to make war with the woman and her seed. It does this by bringing up the beast in his superhuman form.

> The beast has been on the earth in his mortal stage, but as the seventh head he receives a death-wound. Now he comes from the Abyss as the eighth king, comprising all the seven heads and the ten horns. What we saw in Daniel in human form, we now see in super-human form. It is the WHOLE image of Daniel in super-human form; not just one of its mortal parts.

The wild beast is a composite figure with the same features as the dragon; with seven heads and ten horns. This is the same image as in Daniel 7 but in reverse order. Daniel described four wild beasts with seven heads and ten horns among them. The first three beasts were in the east (Daniel 7:7), representing eastern religions. These are likely Mohammedanism, Brahmanism, and Buddhism. The fourth beast is a western religion; probably Christendom. Daniel deals with a phase of earth's religious organization just prior to the emergence of the wild beast.

It appears the earth will be divided into seven divisions; and one of these divisions will be subdivided into ten parts. Some argue that the beast and dragon represent the restored Roman empire; but that empire never ruled all the earth.

Behind the scenes, invisible spirit powers control the course of kingdoms and republics. Men believe they are in control of the destinies of nations, but they are really puppets in the hands of the unseen spirit realm. In Revelation God takes us behind the scenes and shows us Satan's "system" by which everything is operated. The people of earth see a man, and do not know of the power of Satan that is behind everything.

One of the beast's heads appeared as if it had been slain, and the death blow cured. The whole earth marvels after the wild beast.

At least to all appearances Satan brings back to life this one that had been killed. We see here an imitation and distortion of God's work. Just as Christ was crucified and raised again by the power of God, here the wounded head descends into the abyss and is recalled to life by the dragon. Satan deceives by acting in similar fashion with God.

Always in the past Satan had the ability to kill, but not to bring back to life. God gives Satan authority to do so in these ends times to accomplish His purposes. He sends those who have turned against Him an *operation of deception* (2 Thessalonians 2:11) so they will believe a falsehood. This, too, is a part of God's work to accomplish His overall goal.

The human agent used by Satan had been alive previously upon the earth. Now Satan revives him and uses him for his own purposes; raising him to the pinnacle of earthly power.

This beast is not a man that terrorizes men. He is filled with charisma and is most alluring. He promises peace and progress and happiness. Is this not the common belief within the organized church today? Many preachers announce the advent of a great revival to sweep the earth and introduce the kingdom, with peace and happiness.

> # Religion itself (Christendom) is playing into Satan's hand, preparing the way for the man of sin to be introduced and embraced.

They worship the dragon, seeing that it gives authority to the wild beast. They worship the wild beast saying, Who is able to battle with it?

> The theme here is *worship*, not political rule. The religions of the world are apparently conquered by Christendom and melded into a single world religion, worshiping the dragon and the beast. This world religion will persecute those of Israel who are faithful to God.
>
> The false prophet provides signs and calls for worship. But the eonian evangel will call upon men to worship their Creator. (14:7)

The beast speaks great things and blasphemies. It is given authority to do its will for 42 months. It blasphemes God's name and His tabernacle and those tabernacling in heaven.

> Again we see the 3 ½ year period (42 months). In the middle of the 7 year period the beast will break his covenant with Israel and make war against the saints. (Daniel 9:27)
>
> Compare this with 2 Thessalonians 2:4 where Paul warns of this one who is to come, *who opposeth and exalteth himself above all that is called god or that is worshipped; so that he as god sitteth in the temple of God shewing himself that he is God.*

The beast is given to do battle with the saints and to conquer them. Authority is given to it over every tribe and people and language and nation. All who dwell on the earth will worship it, everyone whose name is not written in the scroll of life. Here is the endurance and faith of the saints.

> The three directives for the saints, seen here and throughout Revelation, are flight, patience, and faith.

Another beast comes out of the earth (13:11)

Another wild beast ascends out of the land, with two horns like a lambkin's. It speaks as a dragon. It exercises all the authority of the first beast, making the earth and those dwelling in it to worship the first beast.

> The first beast came from the sea. This second beast comes from the earth. The description of these two (the beast and the false prophet) occupies all of chapter 13.

> The second beast, like the first, is super-human; energized by Satan's power. His mission is to aid the first beast by deceiving mankind. The first beast seems to focus on political power; while the second emphasizes religious power. His miraculous resurrection will be the basis for his demand for worship.

> 2 Thessalonians 2:9 seems to speak of this second beast, whose coming is *according to the working of Satan with all power and signs and lying wonders ... For this cause God shall send them strong delusion, that they should believe the lie.*

Observe ...

MIRACLES ARE NOT EVIDENCE OR PROOF OF DIVINE OR RIGHTEOUS ACTIVITY.

A belief that this is so will play a big part in Satan's ability to deceive.

Some interpreters say these two beasts are simply two aspects of the same thing. And many say these beasts are not individuals. But all Scriptures portray the two as individuals without a hint to an alternate interpretation.

It does great signs; making fire descend out of heaven in the sight of mankind. It deceives those dwelling on the earth because of the signs, telling them to make an image to the first wild beast that had the blow of the sword and lives. It gives spirit to the image of the wild beast, that the image could speak. Whoever is not worshiping the image of the wild beast is killed.

The false prophets perform miracles, as foretold in Matthew 24:24 and 2 Thessalonians 2:9. Conventional wisdom tends to attribute all supernatural occurrences to God, but Satan has authority to use such devices in the end times; and perhaps in our current age as well.

The world has always longed for peace. Many different forms of government have promised peace and have strived for peace, but it is elusive. The false messiah will promise peace. Miracles and demonstrations of power will cause many to support this false messiah, hoping that peace would come at last.

History has never seen myriads receive the emblem, name or number of the wild beast. No religion has had so many followers enlist within such a short span of time. Clearly these events continue to await fulfillment in the future.

It causes all to have an emblem on their right hand or forehead, and no one is able to buy or sell unless they have this emblem of the wild beast, or its name, or the number of its name. The number is the number of mankind; 666.

Most within Israel are safe and nourished, having taken the emblem. But war is being waged upon the faithful remnant. The faithful cannot buy or sell due to this embargo, and they are now totally dependent upon God for provision; reminiscent of the days in the wilderness.

The number seven, used throughout Revelation, denotes perfection, completion, and sufficiency. The number six falls one short of this. Multiplied, 666 is the height of man's futile efforts. Interestingly, 666 has a remarkable property. It is the sum of all numbers from one to the square of six. $1 + 2 + 3 + 4 \dots +36 = 666$.

Observe that there is no provision to be found in Revelation for the protection of the Body of Christ among the nations. Only ISRAEL is addressed. The Body of Christ is not mentioned because it is not present when these things occur. Today, in the 21st Century, the Day of the Lord is imminent; but the coming of Christ for the Body is even MORE imminent.

Now, back to heaven …

CHAPTER 14

The lamb and the 144,000 (14:1)

I saw the Lambkin standing on mount Zion with 144,000 having its name and its Father's name written on their foreheads. A sound came out of heaven as the sound of many waters and loud thunder, and as lyres and singers. They are singing a new song before the throne. No one is able to learn the song except the 144,000 who have been bought from the earth; those not polluted with women for they are celibates. They follow the Lambkin wherever It goes. They are bought from mankind, a firstfruit to God and the Lambkin. They are flawless, with no falsehood in their mouth.

Only those who have gone thru this great tribulation could understand this new song that celebrates their perseverance.

God has always preserved a remnant of the faithful, even in the worst of apostasies. Here the remnant is the 144,000 which will worship God alone, even while all the world is worshiping the wild beast. Their faithfulness will be rewarded when the kingdom is established upon the earth. The apostles will be the leadership in Israel, but among the nations the 144,000 will administer God's government.

Celebates? Fornication would seem to be a part of the great religious system of the Anti-Christ. It will likely become a requirement in the mandatory worship of the beast. Refusal to partake and to give up one's celibacy will result in martyrdom.

The three messengers (14:6)

A messenger is flying in heaven having an *eonian evangel* to bring to those on the earth; to every nation and tribe and language and people; saying with a loud voice, Be afraid of God and give glory to Him, for the hour of His judging came. Worship the Maker of heaven and the land and the sea and the springs of water.

> # The *eonian evangel* is brought to all upon the earth.

As these visions alternate between heaven and earth, John is given God's side of what is going to occur, and then he is told what God is doing during the time the beast and false prophet are at work.

In Matthew 24:14 we were told the *evangel* would be proclaimed worldwide as a testimony to the nations, before the end would come. This *eonian evangel* is not for our current day. It is for the period of time noted here in Revelation; a time of judgement; not grace. It does not ask mankind to *believe*. It tells men to *fear* God, and it demands that only God is to be worshipped; the One Who created the universe! So, this is an evangel of fear, with the hour of judgment having come.

This evangel is not without precedent. Adam and Eve knew God as Creator and Judge. They rightfully feared and hid themselves. In sin, reverential fear is appropriate.

The eonian evangel is a very basic message, with no mention of Christ's blood and redemption. Worship is demanded solely on the basis of His being the Creator. This tells us of the awful state of the earth in these days, where such a primitive evangel is needed.

The 144,000 faithful are sealed and protected in these times, but what about the remainder of Israel who are scattered among the nations? This eonian evangel is addressed to them. Those obedient to this evangel who are martyred are mentioned in verse 13.

We pause here and remember when the Lord, during His earthly ministry, read from Isaiah. (Luke 4:18-20) He read thru a part of the Isaiah passage but then he closed the book and sat down, because it was not yet time to proclaim *the day of vengeance of our God.* But now when the messenger preaches to all the earth, the time has come.

Why were the Thessalonians upset, requiring Paul to console them? A forged letter had arrived, telling them the Day of the Lord had come. (2 Thessalonians 2:2) But since they had not yet been caught up to meet the Lord in the air before that great and terrible Day, they were troubled and distressed. In fact, the Day of the Lord had not yet come; and Paul assured them of such. Here in Revelation, that Day has come.

A second messenger follows saying, It falls! Babylon the great had made all nations drink of the wine of the fury of her prostitution!

Jerusalem is the center and focus for God's people. It is the city chosen by God for His king. Babylon is the center of gentile rule.

Babylon is God's name for the world system controlled by the beast. We saw the Tower of Babel in Genesis 11:1-9, and from that day the Babylonian influence has infiltrated the earth. Jeremiah 51 foretells the fall of Babylon.

A third messenger follows saying, If anyone is worshiping the wild beast and its image and is getting an emblem on his forehead or hand, he also is drinking of God's fury in the cup of His indignation, and he will be tormented in fire and Sulphur.

The fumes of the torment are ascending for the eons of the eons. They have no rest day and night. Here is the endurance of the saints who are keeping the precepts of God and the faith of Jesus.

> Remember, *the eons of the eons* is not of "endless" duration, but is the period of time we now read of in Revelation ... the last two *eons* as compared with ALL of the eons described in the Scriptures.

A voice out of heaven says, Write: Happy are the dead who are dying in the Lord henceforth! They will be resting from their toil, for their acts are following with them.

The harvest (14:14)

I saw a white cloud with One sitting on it like a son of mankind, with a golden wreath and carrying a sharp sickle. Another messenger came out of the temple crying loudly to the One sitting on the cloud, Reap! For the hour came to reap. And the One sitting on the cloud cast His sickle on the earth and reaped.

The hour has arrived for the harvest.

Another messenger came out of the temple in heaven, also carrying a sharp sickle. And another messenger came out of the altar, having jurisdiction over the fire. He cries to the former, Use your sickle and pick the clusters of the earth's grapevine, for its grapes are ripe. And so this is done, and he casts the grapes into the great trough of God's fury. The trough is trodden outside the city, and blood came out of it up to the bits of the horses, for 1600 stadia.

> This is the last time the title "Son of Man" is used. This title always connects the Lord with the earth; not heaven.

CHAPTER 15

Seven angels with seven plagues (15:1)

I saw another sign in heaven, great and marvelous; seven messengers having the last seven calamities. For in them the fury of God is consummated.

I saw a glassy sea mixed with fire. Standing on the sea are the conquerors from the wild beast and its image, with lyres. They are singing the song of Moses and the song of the Lambkin: Great and marvelous are Thy acts, Lord God Almighty. Just and true are Thy ways, King of the eons. You only are good. All the nations will arrive and worship before You.

> All the nations coming to worship points to the completion of judgments, and the commencement of the millennial reign.

> # The kingdom will be setup in Jerusalem, with Christ on the throne. Those of the nations will come into the city to worship.

After this I saw the temple of the tabernacle of the testimony in heaven opened, and out of the temple came the seven messengers with the seven calamities. One of the animals gives each of them a golden bowl brimming with God's fury. The temple is dense with the fumes of God's glory and power. No one was able to enter the temple until the seven calamities were consummated.

> The Tabernacle of Moses and the Temple of Solomon were only copies of the true Tabernacle and Temple in heaven.

CHAPTER 16

Seven bowls of wrath (16:1)

A loud voice told the seven messengers to go and pour out the bowls of God's fury into the land.

> These seven bowls are an expansion of the seventh trumpet. The bowls are poured out on the Jewish worshipers of the wild beast. The seals represent political, economic, and religious problems. The trumpets signal the coming judgment. The bowls are concerned with religion, evidenced

by their being preceded by the opening of the temple. They are the outpouring of God's wrath.

Bowl #1 is poured out on the land: Evil and malignant ulcers come upon those of mankind with the wild beast's emblem and who worship its image.

Previously those worshiping the wild beast were warned there would be no rest day and night. (14:11) Here we see the fulfillment of that warning. There is no rest from pain and distress.

Bowl #2 is poured out into the sea: The sea becomes blood as of a dead man. Every living thing in the sea dies.

Bowl #3 is poured out into the rivers and springs: They become as blood. The messenger of the waters says, You are just, seeing that you judge these. For they shed the blood of saints and prophets. You give them blood to drink, which they deserve.

Bowl #4 is poured out on the sun: It is given to scorch mankind with fire and great heat, and they blaspheme the name of God Who has jurisdiction over these calamities. They do not repent and give Him glory.

Bowl #5 is poured out on the throne of the wild beast: Its kingdom becomes dark and they are in misery. They blaspheme the God of heaven for their miseries and for their ulcers, and they do not repent of their acts.

This bowl initiates a direct attack on the throne of the beast.

Bowl #6 is poured out on the great river Euphrates: Its water is dried up, making ready the road of the kings from the orient. Out of the mouths of the dragon, the wild beast, and the false prophet come three unclean spirits like frogs. These are the spirits of demons, doing signs and going out to the kings of the whole inhabited earth to mobilize them for the battle of the great day of God Almighty.

Lo I am coming as a thief. Happy is he who is watching and keeping his garments, that he may not be walking naked.

The Thessalonian believers were assured that the day would NOT come on them as a thief. (1 Thessalonians 5:4) There Paul wrote to the Body of Christ. Here, with the Body of Christ having been removed, the visions speak of a different time and a different people (Israel) under different conditions (judgement not grace). Here He comes as a thief.

They are mobilized at the place called, in Hebrew, Armageddeon.

Armageddon (or *har-megiddo*) means "the mount of Megiddo." This place was described by Napoleon as the most natural battlefield upon the earth. King Saul lost his life there.

The drying-up of the Euphrates is literal. It will prepare the way for the mobilizing of armies from the orient. The kings of the earth are about to be gathered together to the great battle between heavenly and Satanic and earthly forces. Here the way is cleared for the armies of the east to come.

Bowl #7 is poured out on the air: A loud voice from the temple of God says, It has occurred. There are lightnings and voices and thunders, and a great earthquake such as did not occur since mankind came to be on the earth.

A great earthquake occurred such as did not occur since mankind came to be on the earth. This seems to imply there *had* been major earthquakes or disturbances BEFORE mankind was on the earth. This is also confirmed by geology. We see this when the earth was created and then BECAME a chaos. (Genesis 1:2)

The great city comes to be divided into three parts, and the cities of the nations fall. Babylon the great is given the cup of the fury of God's indignation. Every island flees, and the mountains are not found. Large hail descends out of heaven upon mankind. And men blaspheme God because of this hail, for great is its calamity.

Babylon and the cities of the nations fall.

The seventh bowl, like the seventh trumpet, is a climax; and is immediately followed by the Lord's coming.

Six of the seven bowls are the same as the plagues of Egypt.

The first bowl is like the sixth plague (boils).
The second and third bowls are like the first plague (waters become blood).
The fifth bowl is like the ninth plague (darkness over the land).
The sixth bowl is like the second plague (frogs).
The seventh bowl is like the seventh plague (hail).
Only the fourth bowl has no counterpart in the plagues.

Now let us pause and consider something; for there are some who would say that all the events of Revelation have already taken place in history; many in a figurative way. But can we truly believe we have passed thru this great and terrible Day of the Lord without knowing these extreme conditions and judgments, all the while preaching the evangel of grace as commissioned by Paul?

CHAPTER 17

The woman on the beast (17:1)

One from among the seven messengers came and spoke with me saying, I will be showing you the sentence of the great prostitute who sits on many waters and with whom the kings of the earth commit prostitution, and those dwelling upon the earth are made drunk with the wine of her prostitution.

He carried me away in spirit into a wilderness, and I saw a woman sitting on a scarlet wild beast replete with names of blasphemy, and having seven heads and ten horns.

We will see in verse 18 that this woman is a city. In verse 9 we learn that the seven heads represent seven hills. Interestingly, Rome is built upon seven hills.

The woman was clothed with purple and scarlet and gilded with gold and precious stones and pearls, with a golden cup in her hand brimming with abominations and the uncleanness of her prostitution, and that of the earth. On her forehead was written: Secret. Babylon the Great, the mother of the prostitutes and the abominations of the earth.

The woman's name is a secret sign. It refers to something much deeper than a name itself would convey. And we will soon learn this is not a woman at all, but a city; and not just a city but one that is rife with idolatry.

Babylon is the fountainhead of all idolatry. Satan used Nimrod as the founder of his scheme. Nimrod, in the spirit of anti-Christ, built a city so the people would not be scattered; contrary to God's will. This was rebellion against God. Nimrod called the city Bab-El ("the court of God"), exalting himself.

Babylon is a city, not a system or a religion as some commentators would say. There was a religion instituted by Nimrod at Babylon; though it is not Roman Catholicism (as some would contend).

I saw the woman, drunk with the blood of the saints and the witnesses of Jesus. The messenger said to me, Why do you marvel? I will be declaring to you the *secret* of the woman and of the wild beast with seven heads and ten horns.

John marveled. But what was so unbelievable to generate this response? It seems that all the faiths of the world have merged into a single, unified, Godless cult; Christian, Buddhist, Brahman, and Mohammedan. He sees the woman and the wild beast, and there is no enmity. Even apostate Israel is in unity with God's enemies!

All believe they will enjoy a peaceful millennium; but it is premature and a *false* millennium. Satan is a deceiver and imitator, and he has convinced everyone of his power to deliver what they seek.

The wild beast was, and is not, and is about to be ascending out of the submerged chaos, and to be going away into destruction. Those dwelling on the earth whose names are not written on the scroll of life from the disruption of the world will marvel when they see the wild beast because it was, and is not, and will be present.

The seven heads are seven mountains where the woman is sitting on them, and they are seven kings. Five of them fall, one is, and the other has not yet come. And when he does come he must remain briefly.

The beast is he who has the seven heads and ten horns.

In Daniel the seven kings were successive. Here in Revelation the beast comes up out of the Abyss; superhuman. During the first 3-1/2 years he is mortal, but then he is wounded unto death and returns in superhuman form.

Unlike Daniel, in Revelation the seven heads (or kings) are contemporary, not successive. The beast himself will be the eighth king.

At the time spoken of in verse 10, five of the kings will have fallen. One will be reigning. The seventh will not yet have come. When he does come he will first overthrow the last three of the seven (Daniel 7:8) but will remain only for the first 3 ½ year period. After his death he will be brought back to life by Satanic power. So, in his mortal form he is the seventh king. In his superhuman form he is the eighth king.

Who the five kings will be is not revealed; nor is it necessary for us to know to understand the vision. The seventh we do know; it is the beast in his mortal stage (before he receives the death blow and is subsequently revived by the dragon to become the eighth king).

Some say the kings are as follows:
Five had fallen: Egypt, Assyria, Babylon, Persia, and Greece.
One is present: Rome
One is future: The beast

But the first that was given headship over Israel was Nebuchadnezzar. Dominion was taken from Israel by God and given to the Gentiles (Nebuchadnezzar). Dominion was then passed to Medo-Persia (the second), Greece (the third), Rome (the fourth), and then the present power which succeeded Rome in 646 or 647 AD and is still treading down Jerusalem, or perhaps a future power yet to come (the fifth).

The key to understanding this succession would seem to be headship over Israel. Remember; Israel is the focal point of the events described in Revelation.

The wild beast which was and is not, is the eighth. It is from among the seven, and is going away into destruction.

The eighth will return from the abyss so supreme that he will become sovereign dictator of all nations; the wild beast personified. Immediately after his resurrection he kills the two witnesses (chapter 11).

The ten horns are ten kings who obtained no kingdom as yet but are obtaining authority as kings one hour with the wild beast. These have one opinion, and they are giving their power and authority to the wild beast.

The western head with ten horns is perhaps confederate Christendom. The ten kings probably take power at the same time as subjects of the beast; with the beast becoming the acknowledged leader; having conquered the east. Babylon's plan of concentrating all power in the hands of one man will be fulfilled; and this plays directly into the hand of Satan who has plans of his own.

For Daniel (7:7) the western beast had ten horns which probably represents ten military powers in Christendom. It is easy to grasp how multiple governments might temporarily delegate power to the head of a world league or union of nations that is allegedly guided by Christian values. When the call goes out for an international force to put down the rebellious Jews in Jerusalem who threaten the world government, the federation of nations from west and east will mobilize at Armageddon.

The beast will occupy the City, while the ten kings exercise authority in their own parts of the world.

They will battle with the Lambkin, and the Lambkin will conquer them; as It is Lord of lords and King of kings, and those with It are called and chosen and faithful.

The waters where the prostitute is sitting are peoples and throngs and nations and languages.

The ten horns and the wild beast will be hating the prostitute and will be making her desolate and naked, and they will be eating her flesh and burning her up with fire. For God imparts to their hearts to form *His* opinion and to form one opinion, and to give their kingdom to the wild beast until the words of God shall be accomplished.

While the beast and the kings of the earth are driven by wickedness, still God is in control and is using them to play into His hand, ultimately accomplishing His will. This is much like the Jewish leaders when they plotted to crucify Jesus; carrying out their wicked will while at the same time playing into God's hand.

The woman is the great city which has a kingdom over the kings of the earth.

Again, keep in mind that everything spoken of in Revelation is in relation to Israel. East, west, north or south are relative to Jerusalem. The "heads" denote headship over the people of Israel. The world powers or kingdoms are only considered as they relate to Israel. We tend to place ourselves at the center of things; but Israel is the primary subject of Revelation.

Let us consider the kingdoms and kings in Daniel and Revelation (from "Commentary on Revelation" by E. W. Bullinger):

Daniel	Revelation
Kingdoms	Heads (or Kings)
1. Gold	
2. Silver	
3. Brass	
4. Iron	
5. Clay (or Iron & Clay)	
	"Day of the Lord"
	1. The first Head
	2. The second Head
	3. The third Head
	4. The fourth Head
	5. The fifth Head
	(Five are fallen)
	6. The sixth Head
	(one is; the other is not yet come)
The Great Day of the Lord (The last "week")	
The making of the covenant (Daniel 9:27)	
6. The Kingdom of the beast	7. The seventh Head (mortal)
	("who was, and is not, and shall be present" as the eighth King
"The great and terrible Day of the Lord" (the last half of the "week")	
The breaking of the covenant (Daniel 9:27)	
	8. The eighth King; the beast. (superhuman)
7. "The Kingdom of our Lord and of His Christ."	

CHAPTER 18

The fall of Babylon (18:1)

Another messenger descended out of heaven, having great authority. He cries loudly, It falls! Babylon the great! It became the dwelling place of demons and the jail of every unclean spirit and the cage of every unclean and hateful bird. Because of her prostitution all the nations have fallen. The kings of the earth commit prostitution with her, and the merchants of the earth are rich as a result of her power to indulge.

> All the cities of the nations fall, but a special doom is announced for this one city in particular.
>
> Observe that Babylon does not appear in the early parts of Revelation. It is not connected with the throne; but the temple. It relates to the religious realm.
>
> We learned that the woman is not literally a woman, but a city (17:18). Babylon was the first capital among the nations to rule the world at the beginning of the "time of the gentiles." It will emerge in the end times to rule over the nations.
>
> Commerce today controls the world. This was not so in Rome, which was a military dictatorship. Commerce had not yet been developed.
>
> Some would say this is an accurate description of the USA; wielding broad financial influence around the world and degrading into many sorts of ungodly behavior. While this may be true, we cannot say this passage is prophetically speaking of the USA. BUT; we can learn from these words and understand that which God despises. This should cause us to seek from God's Word those behaviors and acts that He approves of, and those He does not. It is not that we are trying to earn His favor or our salvation, but because of His grace it is simply the right thing to do; the appropriate response on our part.

Another voice out of heaven declares, Come out of her My people, lest you should be joint participants in her sins, and lest you should share in her calamities. For her sins were piled up to heaven and God remembers her injuries.

Pay her double for her acts; for her self-glorification and indulgences. In one day her calamities will be arriving; death and mourning and famine. She will be burned up with fire, for strong is the Lord God Who judges her.

The kings of the earth who commit prostitution and indulge with her will lament and grieve over her when they see the smoke of her burning, standing afar off for fear of her torment. They will say, Woe that great city. Babylon the strong city. For in one hour your judging came.

The merchants of the earth lament and mourn over her, for no one is buying their cargo any longer. All that is sumptuous and splendid have perished from you. The merchants of these things, who are rich through her, will stand afar off because of her torment, lamenting and mourning. Woe! The great city clothed in cambric and purple and scarlet was desolated of her riches in one hour.

The navigators and mariners and whoever work on the sea will observe the smoke of her burning saying, Is there any like this great city? The great city by which all who have ships on the sea are rich, in one hour is desolated.

> According to Bullinger ("Commentary on Revelation"), the Euphrates has long been navigable by ships for 500 miles from its mouth. With little effort it could be navigable by ships of large size.

Make merry over her O heaven, and ye saints and apostles and prophets. For God judges by passing your sentence upon her.

One messenger lifts a large stone, like a millstone, and casts it into the sea saying, Thus Babylon the great city will be hurled down and nevermore found. The sound of lyre singers, entertainers, flutists and trumpeters should be heard in you no more. Every artificer of every trade may be found in you no more. The sound of a millstone should be heard in you no more. The light of a lamp may be seen in you no more. The voice of the bridegroom and bride should be heard in you no more. For your merchants were the magnates of the earth. By your enchantments all nations were deceived. And in it the blood of prophets and saints was found, and all those slain upon the earth.

CHAPTER 19

In heaven ... Hallelujah (19:1)

A loud voice as a vast throng in heaven said, Hallelujah! Salvation and glory and power is of our God, for true and just is His judging. For He judges the great prostitute who corrupts the earth with her prostitution, and avenges the blood of His slaves at her hand.

> The Greek *alleluia* is equivalent to the Hebrew *Hallelu-Jah* (praise ye Jah). The Hebrew occurs only in "the Hallelujah Psalms" and is always in response to the execution of judgment. Here in Revelation it celebrates the destruction of Babylon. There would not seem to be appropriate place

for declaring *hallelujah* in our present day where grace reigns, not judgment.

The 24 elders and four animals fall and worship God Who is sitting on the throne. Again, a loud voice as a vast throng in heaven says, Hallelujah! For the Lord our God Almighty reigns! The wedding of the Lambkin came, and Its bride makes herself ready.

Israel is often referred to as the bride of Jehovah. He became her husband at Sinai. (Jeremiah 31:22) But she forsook Him to pursue other lovers. (Hosea 2:6-13) So He gave her a bill of divorce. (Deuteronomy 24:1-4) Sent into captivity Israel could never be His again according to the law. But nonetheless He invites her to return. (Jeremiah 3:1) He promises to wait for her and to keep her for Himself until the latter days. (Hosea 3:3) During the Lord's earthly ministry He called Israel a wicked and adulterous generation, for they had forsaken God.

How can this be referring to "the Church" that has made herself ready? Members of the Body of Christ are already made ready. (Colossians 1:12) God has made us ready and we are complete in Him. (Colossians 2:10) We cannot be more ready than how He Himself has made us. WE ARE HIS BODY; NOT HIS BRIDE.

We are His Body.
Israel is His Bride.

This marriage is a resuming of God's relationship with Israel.

He said to me, Write: Happy are those invited to the wedding dinner of the Lambkin. I fall at his feet to worship him and he says, No! A fellow slave of yours and of your brethren am I. Worship God!

The wedding feast is described in Matthew 22:10. We recall that some who were extended an invitation refused the garment provided by the host.

The rider on the white horse ^(19:11)

I saw heaven open and a white horse. The One sitting on it is called Faithful and True. In righteousness He is judging and battling. He wears a cloak dipped in blood, and His name is called The Word of God.

> Remember the white horse of the false christ in 6:2. It is now time for the white horse bearing the true Christ to appear.

The armies in heaven follow Him on white horses. Out of His mouth a sharp blade is issuing, that with it He should be smiting the nations. And He will be shepherding with an iron club.

He is treading the wine trough of the fury of God's indignation. And on His cloak and on His thigh a name is written: King of kings and Lord of lords.

> Isaiah 63 provides a vision of this wine trough. At last the sovereignty of Christ as King and Priest is established.

Another messenger cries with a loud voice, saying to all the birds flying in mid-heaven, Be gathered for the great dinner of God, to eat the flesh of kings and captains and the strong, and horses, and those sitting on them.

The wild beast and the kings of the earth and their armies gathered to do battle with Him.

> Men who have subdued the earth now prepare to resist God. They will attempt to shut out the rightful Owner of the earth.

The wild beast is arrested, and also the false prophet who does signs to deceive those getting the emblem of the beast, and those worshiping its image. The two were cast living into the lake of fire burning with Sulphur. The rest were killed with the blade coming out of His mouth. And all the birds are satisfied with their flesh.

> In Daniel 7:9-14 the book was opened, the beast was thrown into the fire, and the Son of Man was given authority.
>
> The beast and false prophet cannot be killed as mere men. They came up from the Abyss, and they now remain alive in the lake of fire at the close of the 1000 years. The armies are mortal and are slain, and their bodies are eaten by the birds of the air.

> # THE RETURN OF THE KING!
>
> # The resistance of mankind is a short battle. Who can withstand the power of God?

CHAPTER 20

The thousand years ^(20:1)

A messenger descends out of heaven with the key of the submerged chaos and a large chain. He binds the dragon, the ancient serpent who is the Adversary and Satan, for 1000 years; casting him into the submerged chaos, locking it, and sealing it, lest he should still deceive the nations before the 1000 years is finished. Afterwards he must be loosed for a little time.

> The identity of this messenger is not important. God saw no reason to reveal the name; and speculation serves no purpose.
>
> Today Satan walks about (1 Peter 5:8), but he will be bound.

Judgement ^(20:4)

I saw thrones, and judgment was granted to those seated on them.

> In Matthew 19:28 we were told of apostles on these thrones. And in Matthew 25:31-46 we saw the foretelling of this judgment.
>
> Judgment often refers to awards and not punishment. Here each will be granted a place in the kingdom as they deserve. It is a setting right of matters. Even the condemnation of the unbeliever is not an exhibiting of God's aimless rage, but is carefully calculated to right all wrongs.

The former resurrection ^(20:4)

The souls of those executed because of the testimony of Jesus and the word of God, and those who do not worship the beast or its image or take the emblem, they also live and reign with Christ 1000 years. This is *the former resurrection.* The rest of the dead do not live until the 1000 years is finished.

> Only those who refuse the sign of the beast will live and reign with Christ for this 1000-year period. The Body of Christ is not found in this resurrection or reigning. (Remember, the Body of Christ was resurrected to life before the events of Revelation commenced. The Body reigns in the heavens – judging messengers as noted in 1 Corinthians 6:3 – while the resurrected Bride-Israel reigns upon the earth during this period.)
>
> The phrase *the rest of the dead do not live until the 1000 years may be finished* is not found in the best manuscript. But the same manuscript also omits the tribe of Gad (7:5) and Simeon (7:7) from the 144,000; so we cannot place too much stress on the omission.

Happy are those having part in the former resurrection. The second death has no jurisdiction over them, and they will be priests of God and of Christ, reigning with Him the 1000 years.

> This is the resurrection of the just (Luke 14:14) and the resurrection of life (John 5:29) in contrast with the resurrection of judgment (20:12). Here we see the fulfillment of the Lord's words, *He that findeth his life shall lose it; and he that loseth his life for my sake shall find it.* (Matthew 10:39; 16:25,6)
>
> The first resurrection is simply the first of two mentioned in this context. It is not the calling on high of Philippians 3:14 or the resurrection of 1 Thessalonians 4:16-17. The "first" simply records the order of events here in Revelation. This first resurrection is what the Old Testament saints looked for. It is the "better resurrection" of Hebrews 11:35.
>
> The millennial reign has to do with religion; not politics. God's priests will minister to the nations and mediate between them and God. In this 1000 years mankind is still estranged from God, and priests are needed to mediate. Man is given a perfect environment, only to discover the lack lies within himself. He will learn that his heart is wrong, even in an ideal environment (as was the case in the Garden of Eden). Freed from deception for 1000 years he should not be susceptible to Satan's deceit; but we will see this is not the case.
>
> Bullinger summarizes the 1000 years as:

The absence of Satan.
The restoration of the earth.
Many physical marvels.
Converting deserts into gardens.
Changes in the sun, moon, and stars that affect the climate and
    fruitfulness of the earth.
Changes in the nature and habits of the wild animals.
Righteous government.
Prolonged life and improved health.

When the 1000 years end, blessedness will not end but will increase with
the glory of the new heavens and the new earth.

The final battle and Satan's doom [(20:7)]

When the 1000 years is finished Satan will be loosed from his jail. He
will come out to deceive all the nations in the four corners of the earth;
Gog and Magog mobilizing for battle. Their number is as the sand of
the sea. They went up over the breadth of the earth, surrounding the
citadel of the saints and the beloved city.

And fire descended from God out of heaven and devoured them.

In the beginning was Satan's first rebellion. Here we see his final
rebellion. In Genesis 1:1 we saw the perfect order and beauty of creation.
But in Genesis 1:2 we see it become ruin and desolate. We are not told
details as to why; but likely it was Satan's first rebellion; prompted by
his pride (1 Timothy 3:6,7). Between Genesis 1:1 and 1:2 Satan becomes a
fallen angel, and the enemy to God and man.

The battle described in Ezekiel 39:17-22 probably occurs here; after the
1000-year reign. Gog and Magog appear to represent the nations in total.
But observe that this entire episode is confined to those *living* in the
nations, and does not speak of a resurrection of the dead.

Man has enjoyed 1000 years of God's goodness. The knowledge of His
goodness has flooded the earth. Man would observe a righteous
government; with peace and prosperity. But these things cannot create a
new heart. The carnal mind is at enmity with God, and is not subject to
the Law of God. So, when Satan is loosed man is quickly deceived and
ready to believe his lies. For man to understand his weakness, Satan HAD
to be loosed for a season.

Since the Tower of Babel man's combining of forces typically is driven by wrong motives and results in calamity. Man tends to believe that thru cooperation great things can be accomplished; but without God. Here we see the height of this thinking. Satan convinces multitudes from all nations to oppose Christ.

This being the case, should we oppose the means used by mankind to "combine forces?" Should we oppose the United Nations, or any form of a league of nations? If we do so thinking we can thwart Satan's plans we are no different from Peter who once intervened and attacked one who had come to apprehend the Lord to prevent His arrest. In that instance the Lord called Peter "Satan," for his actions were attempting to change the course of events God had planned. The events of Revelation, including the rebellion of mankind in opposing Christ, MUST take place. If we work to prevent these events, we work against God; not for Him. Furthermore, we are ambassadors and citizens of heaven, not any nation upon the earth. Ambassadors are not to meddle with the politics of the country to which they are sent.

Before the events of Revelation take place God will withdraw His ambassadors; and with the influence of the ecclesia (Christ's ambassadors) removed, the decline of mankind into total rebellion will occur rapidly.

The Adversary who deceived them was cast into the lake of fire and sulphur, where the beast and the false prophet were also. They will be tormented day and night *for the eons of the eons.*

Not "forever and ever" but for the time period described as *the eons of the eons.* God can surely not become ALL IN ALL (1 Corinthians 15:28) until even these creatures bow before Him and this second death is abolished.

> # Again, the battle is short in this final rebellion. God's will is done!

Judgment of the dead (the great white throne) (20:11)

I saw a great white throne, and He Who was seated upon it was the One from Whose face earth and heaven fled. I saw the dead, the great and small, standing before the throne. Scrolls were opened. And another scroll was opened which was the scroll of life. The dead were judged by that which is written in the scrolls in accord with their acts.

> Observe that this judgement is based upon acts, not faith. Paul's message was justification by faith alone, lest any should boast. That was the message of grace entrusted to him and proclaimed to the Body of Christ. But the Body of Christ was snatched away and called to be with Him in the heavens before the events described in Revelation take place (1 Thessalonians 4:13ff). Now, in Revelation when Christ returns to the earth, judgment is based upon acts.
>
> In God's Word, judgment is not simply the punishment for crime. It is the bringing of justice; the righting of wrongs. Secrets will be exposed, scores settled, and each will receive his due. All will recognize the injustices that took place, and all things will be put right. All will acknowledge God's wisdom and justice, and every knee will bow.

The sea gives up the dead in it, and death and the unseen give up the dead in them. They are condemned, each in accord with their acts. Death and the unseen are cast into the lake of fire. This is the second death; the lake of fire. If anyone is not found written in the scroll of life, he is cast into the lake of fire.

> The scroll of life (book of life in many translations) is specific to Israel. Moses seems to have referred to it when he asks to be blotted out of God's book to save the sinners within Israel (Exodus 32:32). We learned that the conquerors will not have their names erased from the scroll of life (3:5). But those who are not conquerors but who worship the wild beast are not written in the scroll of life (13:8). It is the Israelites who marvel at the wild beast (17:8). Daniel, who speaks of Israel, says those written in the scroll will be delivered (Daniel 12:1). Finally, Paul seems to say that it was his fellow workers of the Circumcision whose names are in the scroll of life (Philippians 4:3). So, this scroll is not a listing of ALL who receive life in this present age of grace. It is specific to ISRAEL where salvation comes thru a mixture of grace and works, and where one's name could be erased based on wrong conduct.

So, the lake of fire now contains everyone, those living at the time and the dead which are raised for judgment. The only exception would be those whose names were written in the book of life, and the Body of Christ which had previously been "changed" (if living) or resurrected (if dead) to meet the Lord in the air (1 Thessalonians 4:13ff).

It is interesting that the only *duration* described for the lake of fire is for Satan, the beast, and the false prophet who will remain there *for the eons of the eons.* Not so with all others. We see they are cast into the lake of fire, but for how long? However long God determines is appropriate and necessary.

The lake of fire is the second <u>death</u>.

Ultimately <u>death</u> (and therefore the lake of fire) will be abolished!
(1 Corinthians 15:21-28)

Since the lake of fire is "the second death" it, too, must be abolished once God's purposes have been completed. The lake of fire, then, is a part of God's process in leading all of His creation to reconciliation.

In God's restoration process, each will acknowledge his sin and the justice in God's judgment. To be reconciled with God one must realize his offenses. The believer in the present age judges himself and is reconciled with God, while the unbeliever is judged by Christ to be reconciled.

CHAPTER 21

The New Jerusalem (21:1)

I saw a new heaven and a new earth, for the former heaven and the former earth pass away, and the sea is no more. And I saw the holy city, new Jerusalem, descending out of heaven from God, made ready as a bride adorned for her husband.

We enter a new eon; the Day of God. 2 Peter 3:7-10 reports that the present heavens and earth will pass away with a booming noise, with the elements dissolved by combustion. The earth and the works in it will be burned up at the coming of the day of God. Isaiah 65:17 promised this new heaven and new earth that was to come.

Observe; the holy city is not heaven itself. It descends OUT OF heaven. The city is heavenly in character, but is to be located upon the earth.

A loud voice from the throne says, The tabernacle of God is with mankind, and He will be tabernacling with them. They will be His peoples, and God Himself will be with them.

He will be brushing away every tear from their eyes. Death will be no more, nor mourning, nor clamor, nor misery. For the former things have passed away.

This is foretold in Isaiah 65:17-19.

He Who is sitting on the throne said, I am making all new! Write, for these sayings are faithful and true. I have become the Alpha and the Omega, the Origin and the Consummation.

To the one thirsting I will give of the spring of the water of life gratuitously. He who is conquering shall be enjoying this allotment. I will be a God to him and he will be a son to Me.

But the timid, the unbelievers, the abominable, murderers, paramours, enchanters, idolaters, and all the false – their part is in the lake burning with fire and Sulphur; the second death. (21:8)

What is the lake of fire; the second death?

Some contend it must be a death just like the first, where one has no consciousness. Others contend it is a figurative death, and that the lake of fire is a purging or a process that prepares the subject for life in God's kingdom. Not much information is provided in Revelation as to these details, but we know enough that we certainly would want to avoid experiencing the second death. And whatever the second death is it is not "forever and ever" but for a period of time. The end result is that God's will is accomplished. Every knee will bow, all will be subjected, all will be reconciled to God, and He will become All in all. (1 Corinthians 15:28)

One of the messengers with the bowls said, I will show you the bride, the wife of the Lambkin.

In the Old Testament, Israel was the wife of Yahweh (Jeremiah 31:32). *Thou shalt not be for another man, so will I be for thee* (Hosea 3). God will not break His word by taking a wife to Himself from the nations. The nations will not take the place of faithful Israel. The nations have no part in the new Jerusalem. Those who receive the Messiah are the bride of the Lambkin (Israel).

He carried me away, in spirit, on a high mountain and showed me the holy city, Jerusalem, as it descended out of heaven. It was luminous like a precious stone, with a wall that is huge and high. It had twelve portals, with twelve messengers at the portals with their names inscribed; which are *THE NAMES OF THE TWELVE TRIBES OF THE SONS OF ISRAEL.* The wall had twelve foundations, and on them were the names of the twelve apostles of the Lambkin.

The names of the twelve tribes and the twelve apostles shows us that this city is for Israel. The twelve have this high honor. Paul, the greatest apostle of them all, is not mentioned. So even at this late date, ISRAEL is the focus; not the nations.

Paul introduced the Body of Christ with no wall or barrier between Jew and Gentile. But the new Jerusalem has nothing to do with the Body of Christ which has long since departed the earth.

The messenger measured the city, its portals, and its wall. The city measured 12,000 stadia, with its length and breadth and height being equal. Its wall measured 144 cubits, made of jasper. The city was clear gold, like clear glass. The foundations were adorned with every precious stone.

This is roughly 1400 miles by 1400 miles, 75% of the size of the United States.

There was no temple, for the Lord God Almighty is its temple, and the Lambkin. The city had no need of the sun or moon, for the glory of God illuminated it, and its lamp is the Lambkin.

The nations will walk by means of its light, and the kings of the earth will carry their glory into it. The portals will not be locked by day, and there will be no night there. They will carry the glory and the honor of the nations into it, but nothing contaminating, nor one who makes an abomination or lie will enter. Only those written in the Lambkin's scroll of life will enter.

> In this "Day of God," righteousness is implanted within the very being of the saints (Israel), but it must be enforced among the nations. Christ will rule with an iron club (Psalm 2:9). Men are still "free" to pursue the desires of their flesh, but there will be penalties for disobedience. While freed from the control of spiritual forces by the binding of Satan, the nations will still be influenced by their own inward corruption. This, too, is a necessary part of God's plan, leading mankind to understand the need for dependence upon God. That is the function of God's government in this final era, administered by Israel. (To see what occurs AFTER this final era, refer to 1 Corinthians 15.)
>
> The saints in Israel will serve as priests for the millennial era. But in the new earth there is no temple. It is not that worship has ceased, but that which was outward will have become inward.

CHAPTER 22

The river of life (22:1)

He showed me a river of water of life issuing out of the throne of God and the Lambkin. In the center of its square and on either side of the river was the log of life, producing twelve fruits in accord with each month. The leaves of the log are for the cure of the nations.

> The tree of life was first seen in Genesis 3:24. Here, in the final eon, we see it again. Those living do not have immortal bodies, but mortal; for the leaves are needed for their cure. If there was unfailing health, if sin was gone, and if the curse was removed, what would be the need for these leaves for *the cure of the nations?*

There will be no more doom, and the throne of God and of the Lambkin will be in it. His slaves will offer divine service to Him. They will see His face, and His name will be on their foreheads. And they will be reigning *for the eons of the eons.*

> THEY will be reigning (His slaves; the faithful of Israel).

They will be reigning FOR THE EONS OF THE EONS The final two eons before God has brought every part of creation into the fold, when every knee is bowing, and when He becomes All in all. We see this happening in 1 Corinthians 15.

So, the leaves of the tree are needed for the cure of the nations, government is still needed to rule, and the second death is still in operation. But as Revelation closes we do not yet see the final state of mankind. Only to Paul was it revealed that which will take place after the conclusion of Revelation; when death is abolished; when every knee will bow; when all are subjected; when Christ has accomplished all that has been assigned to Him and when He turns over the throne to God the Father, and when God at last becomes All in all (1 Corinthians 15).

He is coming (22:6)

He said to me, These sayings are faithful and true. The Lord commissions His messenger to show to His slaves what must occur swiftly. Lo! I am coming swiftly. Happy is he who is keeping the sayings of the prophecy of this scroll.

I, John, am the one hearing and seeing these things. I fell to worship at the feet of the messenger who showed me these things, and he said, No! I am a fellow slave of yours and of your brethren. Worship God!

He told me not to seal these prophetic sayings, for the era is near.

As stated previously, *the era is near* means something different to God than to mankind. For to Him a day is like a thousand years. (2 Peter 3:8)

I am coming swiftly, and My wage is with Me to pay each according to his work.

Remember chapters 2 and 3 and the letters to the seven ecclesias. Here John summarizes those exhortations to good works and faithfulness with a single statement: My wage is with Me, to pay each one as his work is.

I am the Alpha and the Omega, the First and the Last, the Origin and the Consummation. Happy are those who are rinsing their robes, that it will be their license to the log of life, and they may be entering the portals into the city.

Outside are curs, enchanters, paramours, murderers, idolaters, and everyone fabricating and fondling falsehood. (22:15)

> # But were these not destroyed in the second death?

Compare 22:15 with 21:8. It would seem that those "outside" (22:15) are those that are in the lake of fire (21:8). They are *outside* the holy city. Perhaps, then, the second death is a figurative death. (A good book that explores this possibility is *"Journey to and through the Second Death"* by J. Phillip Scranton.)

I, Jesus, send My messenger to testify these things to you in the ecclesias. Let him who is hearing and thirsting come and take the water of life gratuitously.

John's warning (22:18)

If anyone appends to these words, God will append to him the calamities written in this scroll. If anyone should eliminate any words, God will eliminate his part from the log of life and the holy city.

> This curse has no application to the Body of Christ. We have no part in the tree of life or the holy city. Our allotment is celestial, not terrestrial. The calamities written in this scroll are not to fall upon us, for there can be no condemnation for those in Christ Jesus.
>
> Daniel was told to seal up his vision because there was much to occur before its fulfillment. To John, as this era is impending, it is time for these things to be revealed; and for the prophecy to be studied and understood.

CLOSING THOUGHTS

Where is the Body of Christ in Revelation? Always Israel is mentioned in contrast with "the nations," but these nations are clearly not the Body of Christ. Revelation is concerned with *service* and *works*. Those loyal to God are called slaves (2:20). The 144,000 are slaves (7:3). The martyrs are slaves (19:2). John is a slave (1:1). *Sonship* appears to be missing in this period of judgment.

It is my belief, from a study of the Scriptures thru the years, that the Body of Christ will have been removed from the earth *before* the era we read about in Revelation takes place. In 1 Thessalonians 4:17 we see the "snatching away" of those in Christ, and since those in Christ are not to experience the tribulation (1 Thessalonians 1:10) I believe this takes place *before* the events of Revelation. Furthermore, I believe the Body of Christ *must* be removed before the antichrist can be revealed (2 Thessalonians 2:6-8).

What of the last trump? Some claim that the last trumpet in Revelation must be the same trumpet that is heard by those in Christ in 1 Thessalonians 4, but I do not see this interpretation as being correct. The last trumpet in Revelation is simply the last in the *series* of trumpets John sees in the unveiling.

In his "Appendixes to the Companion Bible" E. W. Bullinger makes the following comparisons between Genesis and Revelation.

Genesis	Revelation
The earth created (1:1)	The earth passed away (21:1)
Satan's first rebellion	Satan's final rebellion (20:3,7-10)
Sun, moon, stars for earth's government (1:14-16)	Sun, moon, stars connected with earth's judgment (6:13; 8:12; 16:8)
Sun to govern day (1:16)	No need for the sun (21:23)
Darkness called night (1:5)	No night (22:5)
Waters called seas (1:10)	No more sea (21:1)
A river for earth's blessing (2:10-14)	A river for the New Earth (22:1-2)
Man in God's image (1:26)	Man headed by one in Satan's image (13)
Entrance of sin (3)	Development and end of sin (21,22)
Curse pronounced (3:14,17)	No more curse (22:3)
Death entered (3:19)	No more death (21:4)
Cherubim mentioned in connection with man (3:24)	Cherubim mentioned in connection with man (4:6)
Man driven out of Eden (3:24)	Man restored (22)

Tree of life guarded (3:24)	Right to the Tree of Life (22:14)
Sorrow and suffering enter (3:17)	No more sorrow (21:4)
Man's religion, art, science, resorted to for enjoyment, apart from God (4)	Man's religion, luxury, art, science, in full glory; judged and destroyed by God (18)
Nimrod, a great rebel and king, and hidden anti-God, the founder of Babylon (10:8-9)	The beast, the great rebel, a king and manifested anti-God, the reviver of Babylon (13-18)
A flood from God to destroy an evil generation (6-9)	A flood from Satan to destroy an elect generation (12)
The Bow, token of God's covenant with the earth (9:13)	The Bow, God's remembrance of His covenant with the earth (4:3; 10:1)
Sodom and Egypt, the place of corruption and temptation (13,19)	Sodom and Egypt again; spiritually representing Jerusalem (11:8)
A confederacy against Abraham's people overthrown (14)	A confederacy against Abraham's seed overthrown (12)
Marriage of first Adam (2:18-23)	Marriage of last Adam (19)
Bride sought for Abraham's son (Isaac) and found (24)	A Bride made ready and brought to Abraham's Son (19:9 – see Matthew 1:1)
Two angels acting for God on behalf of His people (19)	Two witnesses acting for God on behalf of His people (11)
A promised seed to possess the gate of his enemies (22:17)	The promised seed coming into possession (11:18)
Man's dominion ceased and Satan's begun (3:24)	Satan's dominion ended, and man's restored (22)
The old serpent causing sin, suffering and death (3:1)	The old serpent bound for 1000 years (20:1-3)
Sun, moon, stars associated with Israel (37:9)	Sun, moon, stars associated again with Israel (12)

Revelation COMPLETES the truths begun in Genesis;

BUT

Revelation is not the final word. While it may occupy the final place in order in the Bible, there is more to follow the events recorded in Revelation. Even as Revelation concludes, mankind is a work in progress.

In his "Commentary on Revelation," E.W. Bullinger notes:

"What we have to look for now is not the conversion of the world, but the judgment of the world. The professing church is deceiving the world. It tells the world that its mission is to improve the world and, by improving its sanitation, housing its poor, and generally preaching the gospel of earthly citizenship, to bring on the millennium, in which no Christ is thought of or wanted! While the majority of the Church's teachers are loudly proclaiming that "the day of the Lord" will not come till the world's conversion comes, the Spirit and truth of God are declaring that the day shall not come until the apostasy comes. (2 Thessalonians 2:3) While the majority of the Church's teachers are maintaining that the world is not yet good enough for Christ, the Spirit is declaring in the Word that the world is not yet *bad* enough."

Coming judgment is the scope of Revelation. It is an unveiling of the awful scenes that will bring all the forces of heaven and earth into conflict that will end *the day of man* and introduce the return of the king and *the Day of the Lord.* In it we see events taking place in the world above and in the world below; a battle between light and darkness; a connection between things unseen and things seen.

Many of the ideas I have shared in this overview are attributed to *"Commentary on Revelation"* by E.W. Bullinger (Kregel Classics), *"The Unveiling of Jesus Christ,"* by A.E. Knoch (Concordant Publishing Concern), and *"Concordant Studies in the Book of Daniel"* by A.E. Knoch (Concordant Publishing Concern). The reader is encouraged to seek out these excellent resources for a more thorough study.

Revelation
The unveiling of Jesus Christ (1:1)
He is coming with clouds and every eye shall be seeing Him (1:7)

Letters to the seven ecclesias   1:11
- Acts, endurance, refusal to bear evil or false teachings, faithfulness unto death, love.
- To those conquering I will be giving authority over the nations (2:26)

In heaven ... worship around the throne   4:1
- The Lambkin is worthy to open the scroll (5:1)

The Seals   6:1
1. False christ comes conquering.
2. War: Peace removed from the earth.
3. Famine.
4. Death to 1/4 of the earth.
5. Martyrs crying for vengeance.
6. Cataclysm.

In heaven ... 144,000 sealed   7:1
- Multitudes in white robes worship (7:9)

The Seventh Seal   8:1
7. Seven trumpets given to seven messengers.
   - Fiery thurible cast from the altar to the earth.
   - Thunder, voices, lightning, earthquakes.

The Trumpets   8:6
1. 1/3 of the earth burned.
2. 1/3 of the sea destroyed.
3. 1/3 of waters made unusable.
4. 1/3 of sun, moon, stars darkened.
5. Scorpion-like locusts released from the submerged chaos – torment for 5 months.
6. 1/3 of mankind killed by four messengers.

Mention of things to come 10:1

- Messenger proclaims that at the 7th Trumpet the secret of God will be consummated (10:1).
- The Temple is measured (11:1).
- Two witnesses will prophesy for 1260 days.

The Seventh Trumpet 11:15

7. "The kingdom of this world became our Lord's and His Christ's, and He shall be reigning for the eons of the eons."

A great sign in heaven 12:1

- A woman ready to give birth.
- A dragon drags 1/3 of the stars to earth, waiting to devour the child.
- The child is snatched away to God.
- The woman flees and is protected for 1260 days.
- A battle in heaven; the dragon is cast down to the earth.
- The dragon persecutes the woman, but she is protected & nourished for 3 ½ years.

The beast 13:1

- A beast ascends from the sea.
- The dragon gives it power and throne and authority.
- The earth marvels at the beast, that appears as slain and cured.
- They worship the dragon and the beast.
- The beast is given authority for 42 months.
- Another beast ascends out of the land, using signs to cause all to worship the first beast.
- All not worshipping the image of the beast are killed.
- All are forced to receive the emblem of the beast.

In heaven ... 144,000 sealed 14:1

- The 144,000 follow the Lambkin wherever It goes.

Messengers 14:6

- A messenger brings an *eonian evangel* to those on the earth: *"Fear God & worship Him."*
- A messenger proclaims the fall of Babylon.
- A messenger warns those taking the emblem of the beast.
- A messenger announces: The hour has come to reap.
- One like a son of mankind reaps.

Seven messengers with seven plagues 15:1

1. Bowl #1: Evil & malignant ulcers on those with the beast's emblem.
2. Bowl #2: Sea becomes blood; everything dies.
3. Bowl #3: Rivers & springs become as blood.
4. Bowl #4: Sun scorches mankind with great heat.
5. Bowl #5: The beast's kingdom becomes dark and in misery.
6. Bowl #6: The Euphrates is dried up.
   - The kings of the earth are mobilized by the dragon, beast, and false prophet.
7. Bowl #7: Lightning, voices, thunder, great earthquake, cities of the nations fall, great hail.

The woman on the beast 17:1

- Woman: Babylon the Great, the mother of prostitutes and abomination.
- Wild beast: Was, is not, about to be ascending out of the submerged chaos.
- 7 heads: 7 kings. 5 fall, one is, one has not yet come.
- The wild beast is the 8th king.
- 10 horns: 10 kings that will obtain authority briefly with the wild beast.
- They will battle and be conquered by the Lambkin.
- 10 horns & the beast will hate the prostitute and will make her desolate & naked.

The fall of Babylon 18:1

- Nations have fallen because of her prostitution.
- Merchants & kings grieve over her.
- In one hour her judging came.
- Rejoicing in heaven.

The rider on the white horse 19:11

- The armies in heaven follow Him on white horses.
- The beast and the kings of the earth gather to battle Him.
- The beast & false prophet are cast into the lake of fire.
- The rest are killed.
- The dragon is bound for 1000 years (20:1).
- Thrones & judgment (20:4).
- The former resurrection (20:4).
- They reign with Christ 1000 years.

The final battle   20:7
- Satan loosed after 1000 years.
- He deceives the nations & mobilizes armies that surround the city.
- Fire descends from heaven & devours them.
- The Adversary is cast into the lake of fire *for the eons of the eons.*

White throne judgment   20:11
- The dead are judged according to their acts.
- Any not in the scroll of life are cast into the lake of fire.

The New Jerusalem   21:1
- Descends out of heaven.
- The timid, unbelievers, abominable, murderers, paramours, enchanters, idolaters are in the lake of fire (the second death).
- 12 portals inscribed with the names of the 12 tribes of Israel.
- Kings of the earth will carry their glory into the city.
- River of life ... tree of life.
- Outside are curs, enchanters, paramours, murderers, idolaters.

Israel is specifically mentioned throughout.
No mention of the Body of Christ.
"Nations" always contrasted with Israel.
"Nations" is clearly not the Body of Christ.
Even at the end: 12 Tribes (21:12), 12 apostles (21:14).

The Consummation

As Revelation comes to an end, we see the end of the ages. But as the last "Amen" of Revelation 22 is uttered, there is more to come. The crowning event of the ages is found in 1 Corinthians 15, the "consummation" of the ages. Many believe the end of Revelation is a description of the eternal heavens that we will experience when the resurrection takes place. But there are numerous reasons to conclude that this is not the case, and that 1 Corinthians 15 happens after the end of Revelation 22.

Revelation	1 Corinthians
The slaves of God are reigning (22:5) There are still "kings of the earth" (21:24)	All sovereignty, authority and power nullified (15:24)
Christ is seated on the throne (21:5)	Christ must reign UNTIL He places all enemies under His feet (15:25)
	When All is subject to Christ, He subjects Himself to God (15:28)
	All sovereignty, authority, power nullified (15:24)
Lake of fire (second death) still exists (21:8)	Last enemy (death) abolished (15:27)
Leaves on the tree for "the cure of the nations" implies corruptible bodies needing the leaves to sustain life (22:2)	Incorruptible, spiritual body (15:42-44)
Twelve tribes (21:12) Twelve apostles (21:14) Nations outside city (21:24)	No Jewish connotations in 1 Corinthians 15. No barrier between Jew and Greek in Paul's writings.
All speaks of a physical place upon the earth with mortal bodies; much like our present world but with Christ reigning and keeping evil out (22:14-15)	Paul describes a spiritual realm with no corruption, no reign, no power. All are subjected. There are no enemies, sin, or rebellion. The purpose of the ages has been achieved. God is All in all. (How could He be All in all with death, the enemy, still present?)
Revelation describes the final age/eon.	Paul describes "The Consummation" which occurs after the ages/eons have been completed.

In Revelation 21:1 John perceives "a new heaven and a new earth", and he sees "the holy city, new Jerusalem, descending _out of heaven._" The New Jerusalem is not heaven itself, but it descends _out of heaven_.

Appendix

Key Words & Phrases in the Scriptures

I offer here some basic explanations of key terms and concepts, with some limited references. The reader is encouraged to use these comments as points to think about, and to embark on a detailed biblical study of these key topics. Use the Keyword Concordance at the back of your Concordant Literal New Testament to examine every instance where these words and phrases appear in the Greek.

Keep in mind that this represents my own understanding after having studied the Scriptures for many years. I am a life-long <u>student</u> of the Scriptures and what follows represents my current understandings, recognizing that Biblical study is continually a work in progress. Some things in the Scriptures are very clear, and an accurate understanding will not change as study continues. But other things are less clear, and we must simply endeavor to understand as accurately as possible that which God has revealed to us. Let us never think that we have arrived and that we know more than others with different understandings. Instead, let us work together within the Body of Christ as we attempt together to reach an accurate understanding of that which God has revealed.

Consider the opinions of others, but do not give too much credence to ANY man or woman, regardless of their reputation or stature as a preacher, teacher, scholar, or author. I encourage the reader always to study and think for himself.

<u>All in All</u>

It is God's ultimate plan to become *All in all*. All will be subjected to and reconciled to Him. Currently God may be All in some, but He will one day be All in all.

Christ is *the One <u>completing</u> the all in all* (Ephesians 1:23). It is through Christ that all are being reconciled to God (Colossians 1:20). The Body of Christ is the <u>complement</u> of Christ (Ephesians 4:14); *the complement of the One completing the all in all* (Ephesians 1:23).

Our "Great Commission" is found in 2 Corinthians 5:18-21. We are to proclaim the message of reconciliation to God. [Note: Matthew 28 which is commonly referred to as "The Great Commission" was directed to Israel, not to the Body of Christ.]

We see God finally becoming All in all (1 Corinthians 15:28) once Christ has accomplished His mission to bring all into subjection. In 1 Corinthians

15:22-28 there is no longer any need for sovereignties or authorities, and the final enemy (death) is abolished as God becomes All in all. If the lake of fire (the second death) was still burning, all would not yet be <u>reconciled</u> to God, and God would not yet be All in all. In this world we see chaos and tribulation all around us, but things will not always be in this state. God is in the process of becoming All in all.

Believer

A "believer" is simply one who *believes* God. Abraham believed God, and it was reckoned to him as righteousness. We are not provided with an exhaustive list of exactly what Abraham believed, and some of his decisions seemed to display a degree of misunderstanding as to what God had in mind (e.g. fathering a son through Hagar, instead of waiting on God to deliver Isaac through Sarah). But whatever the specifics, we simply read that Abraham *believed* God and it was reckoned as righteousness.

Churches today like to create lists of what one must believe to be a Christian. These lists vary from one church to another, and this should tell us something. Some say we must believe in the doctrine of the Trinity. Others say we must believe that hell is eternal. Some say we must be water baptized. Some even specify the precise mode of water baptism. The problem is that we are often driven by the fear of what God will do to us if we don't believe all of the right things. One slip, and we think that makes us a non-believer and destined for eternal torment. We are thinking in terms of what we must believe, at a minimum, to be "saved." We place no real trust in God and His grace. We think we must <u>do</u> something to be saved, even if this <u>doing</u> is simply mustering-up the right formula of belief.

But there is not really a formula or list of what one must believe. The fact is that through God's Word, and through the person of His Son, God has spoken. We are asked to *believe*; period. We don't fully understand all details, and some understand more details than others, but we are not asked to fully understand all details of God's revelation; only to *believe*.

Here's something else to think about. If believing was something we could muster-up on our own we could boast about that, couldn't we? I could say I am smarter than those who don't believe since I have the intelligence to believe while they do not. But aren't we told that salvation is a gift from God, lest any should boast? (Ephesians 2:9)

I don't think *anyone* could be a believer unless God *enables* that person to believe. Without God's help, the entire world would be non-believers destined for God's judgment. But rather than abandon this hopeless lot called humanity, God chooses _SOME_ and enables them to believe, not because He loves them more but because He has a purpose for them that will ultimately lead to _ALL_ being reconciled to God. This is God's method; to choose _SOME_ to act as His instruments so that _ALL_ will ultimately be reconciled to Him. After all it is God's will that all mankind be saved (1 Timothy 2:4), and He is operating all in accord with the counsel of His will (Ephesians 1:11).

If you think that every person has the ability, on his own, to become a believer by having enough intelligence to believe, consider the following:

✓ The apprehensions of the unbelievers are blinded by the god of this eon (Satan). (2 Corinthians 4:3)

✓ To the Philippians belief on Christ was "graciously granted." (Philippians 1:29)

✓ Not one is just; not one is understanding; not one is seeking out God. (Romans 3:10-11)

With all of this being true, is it even possible for a single person to believe on their own? Or, like Lydia (Acts 16:14), are we dependent upon God to open up our heart to believe?

A "non-believer" is one who does not believe. Doubting Thomas is a good example. Thomas knew what Jesus had said about His approaching resurrection, just as the other apostles. Upon hearing the testimony of those returning from the empty tomb, the others believed. But not Thomas. He would not believe until he could see for himself, and touch Jesus. Did Jesus cast him away for his failure to believe? No; He allowed Thomas to see and touch Him.

Some will believe in this current lifetime, by faith. Others will not believe until they can see for themselves. But one way or the other, there will come a day when every knee will bow before the Lord, and when all are reconciled to God the Father.

Believers, Purpose of

Why has God chosen a certain, select group from mankind (the Body of Christ in this present age)?

✓ To make known the secret of His will ... to head up all in the Christ. (Ephesians 1:9-10)

- ✓ To serve as the complement of the One completing the All in all ... i.e. Christ's complement. (Ephesians 1:23)

- ✓ To be Christ's ambassadors, as if God were entreating through us. (2 Corinthians 5:18-21) To assist in bringing about God's becoming All in all, through the faithful proclamation of the evangel in this capacity of ambassadors.

- ✓ In the oncoming eons to be a display of the riches of God's grace and kindness. (Ephesians 2:7) In other words; God has chosen the Body of Christ so that the glory of His grace might be made known throughout the entire universe.

- ✓ Created in Christ Jesus (as His Body) for good works which God makes ready beforehand, that we should be walking in them. (Ephesians 2:10)

- ✓ To make known to the sovereignties and the authorities among the celestials, the multifarious wisdom of God ... (Ephesians 3:8-11)

- ✓ To make all grow into Him, Who is the Head – Christ. (Ephesians 4:15-16)

What makes this group different from the rest of mankind?

- ✓ All mankind may hear the word of God, but the word of God is *operating* in the believer. (1 Thessalonians 2:13)

- ✓ The believer has *expectation;* a knowledge with certainty as to what will occur in the ages to come ... the *resurrection.* (1 Thessalonians 4:13)

Blaspheme

From the Greek word *blasphemos.* When used of God, translators will use the English *blaspheme.* But the same word is often used of others, in which case translators will use *calumniate,* or something similar. The word simply means "to speak against in a negative fashion."

Church

See "Ecclesia"

Day

Three different days are noted in the Scriptures.

Paul refers to our present day as *man's day* or the *day of man.* (1 Corinthians 4:3) This is a day to which Paul has no desire to conform. During this era man displays what he is not capable of accomplishing on his own. No matter what the circumstance, the form of government (even democracy) or the creation of well-intentioned laws, there is continued failure. Man's day will come to a close when the Day of the Lord arrives, but it must last long enough to allow humanity to prove its inabilities.

The Lord's Day (Revelation 1:10) is thought to be Sunday, the "Christian sabbath." But the Bible speaks of no such thing as a Christian sabbath. The sabbath, being the seventh day, was given to the Jew to observe as a part of the law. It is only because Christians seek to substitute themselves for Israel throughout the Scriptures that we have this confusion. In this present age there is no such day designated as "the Lord's day." This is a fabrication of man's traditions. "The Lord's day" instead refers to a time not yet here, when "man's day" will cease and when the "Lord's day" will begin. To John it was given to experience *the Lord's day* so as to bring the revelation of Christ to mankind.

The *Day of the Lord* (Acts 2:20; 1 Corinthians 5:5; 1 Thessalonians 5:2; 2 Thessalonians 2:2; 2 Peter 3:10) is simply a linguistic variation of *The Lord's Day*. There is no difference in meaning between these variations; the linguistic difference is for the purpose of emphasis. The prophets emphasized the character of the day that was to come (the Day of the Lord), while John emphasizes the Lord as He is unveiled and exalted (the Lord's day). The Scriptures speak often of the Day of the Lord. The Day of the Lord, into which John finds himself transported in his vision, is the time foretold by the prophets.

God's Day (2 Peter 3:12) or the *Day of God* (Revelation 16:14) is the day when God will be exalted on the new earth.

It would seem that the common theme to each of these days is *exaltation*. Man has exalted himself in the *day of man*. When the Lord returns, He will be exalted in the *Day of the Lord*. And ultimately God will be exalted in *God's Day*.

Day of the Lord / Coming Indignation

The Day of the Lord is that period of time following the removal of the Body of Christ unto the heavens (1 Thessalonians 4:13ff) when the events immediately preceding and culminating with the return of Christ to the earth will take place.

Consider the sequence of events as revealed in the Scriptures. John the Baptist spoke of fleeing from the impending indignation, calling upon his audience (Israel) to produce fruit worthy of repentance. But when Paul introduced God's revelation for this present era he announced that God was in Christ conciliating the world to Himself, not reckoning mankind's offenses to them. Far from a message warning of impending indignation, Paul announced that God was <u>conciliated</u> to mankind. Our message, as Christ's ambassadors, is simply: *Be conciliated to God.* (2 Corinthians 5:18-21)

Most certainly there will come a time when God's indignation will come (Romans 2:9), on the *day of indignation* that is set by God. (Romans 2:5) But the believer is saved from this coming indignation (Romans 5:9) by *our Rescuer out of the coming indignation* (1 Thessalonians 1:10). We within the Body of Christ are saved from the coming indignation not because we are better than others of humanity; but because God has elected to choose a subset of humanity; giving them the ability to believe and perceive that which He has revealed; and enabling them to serve as a complement of Christ in this age and in the ages to come; toward the end that God's will for mankind be accomplished; that all mankind be saved and come to a realization of the truth. (1 Timothy 2:4)

But before indignation comes upon the earth, Christ will descend from heaven and *snatch away* the Body of Christ. This event, described in 1 Thessalonians 4:13-18, is commonly referred to as the rapture. When Paul speaks of a *detainer* that must be removed before the man of lawlessness can be unveiled (2 Thessalonians 2:6-12), it would seem that this detainer is the Body of Christ – or more probably the holy spirit that dwells within the Body of Christ -- that is indeed removed on the day that Christ descends. Once the detainer is removed, the man of lawlessness is revealed, and the day of indignation will arrive, as described in the book of Revelation.

Death

The Greek philosophers have us convinced that our souls are immortal. But we are told that only Christ is immortal. (1 Timothy 6:16) When we die our body returns to the soil and our spirit returns to God Who gave it. (Ecclesiastes 12:7) But our soul, which was generated when God animated the soil with His spirit, goes to an *unseen place.* The word in Greek is *hades*, and in the Hebrew it is *sheol.*

Convinced that we are immortal and that our soul must be accounted for, most Bible translators use *hell* for hades if the passage refers to one who is wicked, or *grave* if the passage refers to one who is righteous. But the fact is that every person, righteous or wicked, goes to *hades*; the unseen place. There we will have no consciousness (Ecclesiastes 9:5; Psalm 6:5). This is why those who are dead are sometimes referred to as asleep, where we also have no consciousness. We are totally dependent upon God to resurrect us, as He has promised to do. At the time we are resurrected we will *put on immortality* (1 Corinthians 15:53-54).

Some will object, pointing to passages such as Luke 23:43 when Jesus tells the thief on the cross beside Him, *I say to you, today you will be with Me in paradise.* But all such passages are either mistranslated or misinterpreted, because the translator believes we are immortal and renders the translation with that bias. As for Luke 23:43, since there is no punctuation in the original Greek the placement of the comma in this sentence is an interpretation. Based on what we know from elsewhere in the Scriptures about death, the passage should have been translated: *I say to you today, you will be with Me in paradise.*

Others will object: "Are you saying my loved one is not in heaven right now?" Personally, I am comforted just as much knowing that my loved ones are asleep, and that the next conscious moment they experience will be with the Lord. Furthermore, what becomes of us is not determined by our own wishes or desires but by God Who created us and Who is in full control of our destinies.

Devoutness / Reverence

Devoutness is an important trait to be found in the believer. Consider the number of times Paul emphasizes it in 2 Timothy alone. If we examine every instance where the Greek root *seb* is found in the New Testament, we find it is best translated "revere" in the verb form, "reverence" in the noun form, and "devout" when used as a human characteristic. To be devout is to properly revere God. This notion is somewhat confused in most English translations where we see a variety of word choices such as devout, godly, godliness, worship, piety, and holiness. If the word is consistently translated "revere" or "devout" we will have a better understanding of the desired attitude of revering God.

Disruption

The Greek *katabole* is rendered "foundation" in most modern English translations. It should be translated "disruption" ... *kata* (down) *bole* (cast). Bole (cast) suggests a forcible motion: "hewn down and *cast* into the fire." (Matthew 3:10) The Greek stem "kata bal" is used in the Septuagint (the Greek translation of the Old Testament which existed in the days of Jesus) to translate nine difference Hebrew words, all having the idea of "cast", "break down", "ruin", etc.

The earth was not created in a chaotic state; it *became* a chaos. "He did not create it a chaos." (Isaiah 45:18)

"In the beginning God created the heaven and the earth. And the earth <u>was</u> without form, and void ..." (Genesis 1:1-2 ... KJV) The Concordant Version (a very literal translation) reads: "Created by the Elohim (plural) were the heavens and the earth. Yet the earth BECAME a chaos and vacant ..."

Here we find the *causative* form of the verb "be" (*eithe*). Most translations ignore the causative and act as if there were no verb in the Hebrew. The simple form of the verb of existence need not be expressed; its absence would plainly imply "was" (The earth "was" without form ...). The presence of the causative form of the verb tells us the earth was *caused* to be a chaos and vacant. This is the same as in Genesis 1:3 where the causative verb is also found, and is translated *"Let there be* light", and not "The light was."

Notice the reference to an ancient earth *cohering out of water;* "There were heavens of old, and an earth cohering out of water and through water, by the word of God; through which the then world, being deluged by water, perished." (2 Peter 3:5-6) This could possibly refer to the flood in Noah's day, but would this really be considered "heavens of old" and "an earth cohering out of water and through water"? It sounds more like the chaos conditions that existed at the time of Genesis 1:9 ... "Flow together shall the water from under the heavens to one place, and appear shall the dry land."

Let us look at passages that refer to a "disruption":

John 17:24-25: Jesus speaking; "for Thou lovest Me before the *disruption* of the world." (KJV: *"foundation* of the world" -- NIV: *"creation* of the world")

Eph 1:3-4: "He chooses us in Him before the *disruption* of the world." (KJV: *"foundation* of the world" -- NIV: *"creation* of the world")

1 Peter 1:19-21: "... the precious blood of Christ, as of a flawless and unspotted lamb, foreknown, indeed, before the *disruption* of the world..." (KJV: *"foundation* of the world" -- NIV: *"creation* of the world")

We find the verb form of "katabole" in Hebrews 6:1 -- "... we should be brought on to maturity, not again *disrupting* the foundation of repentance from dead works ..." (KJV: "not *laying again* the foundation" -- NIV: "not *laying again* the foundation") This is a very interesting verse, since both *disruption* and *foundation* are found in the same verse. Here *foundation* comes from the Greek "themelioo" (place-care), which is clearly different from *disruption*. But most modern English translators will use "foundation" for the Greek "katabole" in the aforementioned verses.

The inconsistency of most translators is revealed by 2 Corinthians 4:9 where even our English translators see "kataballo" as a form of disruption: "*cast down*, but not destroyed" (KJV) -- "*struck down*, but not destroyed" (NIV)

How can the same Greek word mean both "foundation" or "creation" and "cast down?" Don't these appear to be opposites; and from the same Greek word?

What are the implications of all of this? If we choose to enter into the creationism/evolution debate using the Bible as our standard, we must consider that the earth could be much older than 6,000 years, and that this is still consistent with what the Bible says (when properly translated). The earth could have been created long before, and then in Genesis 1:2 it *became* chaos. The original created earth has been through a *disruption*, when it *became* chaos.

Before we take a stand based on what the Bible says, we must be sure what it really does say. There is a need for a close study of God's Word, using a good literal translation, not one that is simply easy to read, or that our own personal history has led us to accept as our favorite. The Concordant Version is one of the few English translations that were scientifically prepared, striving for consistency in the translation and avoiding the bias of the translators.

Some scholars will defend the translation, "The earth was without form and void". But we must accept that there is at least the *possibility* that the Hebrew is intended to convey "the earth *became* a chaos and vacant" and there COULD therefore have been a gap, either short or long in duration, between Genesis 1:1 and 1:3.

For more detailed study, see "Unsearchable Riches" magazine, published by Concordant Publishing Concern, January 1957 (Volume 48 Number 1) and May 1957 (Volume 48 Number 3). We also recommend "Without Form & Void" by Arthur Custance.

Ecclesia

The Greek *ecclesia* is most always translated *church* in our Bible versions, except in those cases where the notion of *church* does not fit. This inconsistency in translation causes us to lose valuable insights provided by God, and requires that we place great faith in the translators and not in the word of God itself.

Most within the organized church today insist that Matthew 16:13 represents the beginning of the church, as it is typically translated *upon this rock will I be building my church.* Again, the Greek *ekklesia* simply means <u>called-out-ones</u> (*ek* – out; *klesia* – called). If we examine *ekklesia* in every instance where it is found we will see that it does not always refer to the same group of called-out-ones in every case. It is used to refer to an assembly in Moses' day (Acts 7:38), an unruly mob (Acts 19:32), and a legal assembly like a jury (Acts 19:39). An ecclesia is simply a group of people *called out* from the general masses for a particular purpose. Even in cases where ecclesia is a group that God has *called out,* can we assume it is always the same group (i.e. today's church)? Those called out in Jesus' day and in the book of Acts were exclusively Jewish believers whose expectation was the kingdom from heaven to come upon the earth. But those called out in Paul's day were Jews and Gentiles alike called into one "body," whose expectation is in the heavenly realm. (1 Thessalonians 4:13) Therefore when Jesus proclaims to Peter, *On this rock will I build My ecclesia,* He speaks of the out-called Jews who are hearing the kingdom evangel and who are preparing for the kingdom to be established upon the earth, as it had been in David's day.

There is a big difference between the church we see in Acts which is wholly comprised of Israelites, and the church that Paul speaks of which is comprised of Jew and Gentile alike with no distinction.

Consider the church in the book of Acts:

> *"Men! Israelites! Hear these words ..."* (Acts 2:22)

> *"Let all the house of Israel know ..."* (Acts 2:36)

> *"Those indeed, then, who are dispersed from the affliction which is occurring over Stephen, passed through as far as Phoenicia and Cyprus and Antioch, speaking the word to no one except to Jews only."* (Acts 11:19)

Later in Acts, Paul announces he will turn to those of the nations, since Israel had rejected the gospel. *To you first was it necessary that the word of God be spoken. Yet, since, in fact, you are thrusting it away, and are judging yourselves not worthy of eonian life, lo! we are turning to the nations.* (Acts 13:46) But even then, Paul would go first to the synagogues to address the Israelites.

"... *they came to Thessalonica, where there was a synagogue of the Jews. Now, as was Paul's custom, he entered to them, and on three sabbaths he argues with them from the scriptures ...*" (Acts 17:1)

"*Now he argued in the synagogue on every sabbath ...*" (Acts 18:4)

"*Now it occurred three days after, that he calls together those who are foremost of the Jews.*" (Acts 28:17)

Until, at the very end of Acts, Paul announces: *Let it be known to you, then, that to the nations was dispatched this salvation of God, and they will hear.* (Acts 28:28)

We remember that Paul was entrusted with the evangel of the Uncircumcision, and to Peter was entrusted the evangel of the Circumcision (Galatians 2:7). We have observed that through the book of Acts those receiving the Word of God were those of Israel. This makes perfect sense, since the message being proclaimed pertained to the kingdom that would be restored unto Israel as promised by the prophets of old. *Repent, then, and turn about for the erasure of your sins, so that seasons of refreshing should be coming from the face of the Lord, and He should dispatch the One fixed upon before for you, Christ Jesus, Whom heaven must indeed receive until the times of restoration of all* (Acts 3:19).

Israel awaited the coming of the Messiah who would reign on David's throne, restoring the kingdom to Israel. And thru Israel, all nations would be blessed. This was the message proclaimed to the ecclesia by Peter and the Twelve. And the ecclesia were Jewish believers.

But consider the ecclesia that Paul spoke of:

"*For there is no distinction between Jew and Greek.*" (Romans 10:12).

"*Yet all the members of the one body, being many, are one body, thus also is the Christ. For in one spirit also we all are baptized into one body, whether Jew or Greeks, whether slaves or free, and all are made to imbibe one spirit.*" (1 Corinthians 12:12)

"*For whoever are baptized into Christ, put on Christ, in Whom there is no Jew nor yet Greek, there is no slave nor yet free, there is no male and female, for you all are one in Christ Jesus.*" (Galatians 3:27)

Peter, having been entrusted with the evangel of the Circumcision, spoke to the ecclesia comprised of believers out of Israel. Paul, having been entrusted with the evangel of the Uncircumcision, spoke to the ecclesia comprised of believers out of the nations. He later taught, in his letters, concerning the Body of Christ; comprised of Jew and Gentile without distinction.

Should we be mixing these ecclesias together, assuming they are the same? Would it not be better to simply transliterate the Greek ekklesia as ecclesia ("called-out-ones") in our Bible translations, allowing the Bible student to discern from each instance who the called out ones are?

Ecclesia simply means called-out-ones; those who are called out from the larger group of humanity for some specific purpose. But just as there are different presidential administrations with different policies in our political realm, so also there are different administrations in God's workings in the world. In his letters, Paul speaks of the specific administration of God that was granted to him, in which the Body of Christ is the *ecclesia*, or group of called-out-ones, for which he became a dispenser of good news. The Body of Christ was not introduced by any other person in the Scriptures, either before or after Paul. This was Paul's commission. Peter and others of the Twelve addressed the believers AMONG ISRAEL; that was the called-out-group (ecclesia) they addressed. Paul had a *different* commission, in a *different* administration, and the Body of Christ was the called-out-group (*ecclesia*) that he addressed.

Whenever you see the word *church* in your translation, remember the underlying Greek *ecclesia* simply means called-out-ones; and the group of called-out-ones may vary from one passage to another.

Eon / Eonian

This is one of the most misunderstood words in the Bible. The Greek word *aion* and its Hebrew equivalent *olam* clearly do not mean endless or eternal, but refer to fixed periods of time with a beginning and an end. Thus the many variations we see in the Scriptures:

- ✓ Eon (singular)
- ✓ Eons (plural)
- ✓ Before the eons
- ✓ End of the eon (singular)
- ✓ End of the eons (plural)
- ✓ Eon of the eons
- ✓ Eons of the eons

- ✓ The oncoming eons
- ✓ The impending eon
- ✓ This eon
- ✓ The current eon

There is much said about this present eon (not surprising since this is the eon most of the Scriptures are focused on). It is interesting that nothing good is said about *this* eon. It is a wicked eon. (Galatians 1:4) There is a wisdom of this eon and it is in the chief men of this eon; men who crucify the Lord. (1 Corinthians 2:6-8) There is a god of this eon who opposes Christ and the evangel. (2 Corinthians 4:3-6)

Most Bible translations treat the Greek *aion* in its various forms very inconsistently, sometimes using *eternal* and other times *age* when eternal will not fit. But such inconsistent handling of the word causes much of what God has revealed to us to be lost or confused. The adjective form *eonian* refers to something that takes place during one eon, or during several eons.

Some believe that phrases acclaiming Christ as *King of the eons* (1 Timothy 1:17) prove that eons must mean eternal, since Christ is immortal. I have five children; Cris, Dusty, Chad, Kari and Scott. When I find myself in the midst of Chad's friends I may say, "I am the father of Chad." Does this mean I am not also the father of my other four children? No; but when in the context of Chad's friends, I may identify myself as Chad's father. Likewise, within the context of the eons ... these finite periods of time in which man's history is recorded in the Scriptures ... Christ who is immortal may be described as the *King of the eons*.

Well known and respected preacher and author G. Campbell Morgan expressed it best, noting there is no word in the Greek that translates to our English word *eternal* and which means endless. When God is described as an *Eonian God* this does not mean He is not, in fact, eternal. It is just that the Bible talks about things as they exist or occur in this time period known as the eons. God is eonian, though He will also continue to exist after the eons are concluded.

Following is a listing of where "aion" can be found in its various forms.

"BEFORE THE EONS"
- ✓ 2 Timothy 1:9-10
- ✓ Titus 1:1-3
- ✓ 1 Corinthians 2:6-8

"THIS EON" *(Singular)*
- ✓ Matthew 12:32
- ✓ Matthew 13:22
- ✓ Mark 4:19
- ✓ Luke 16:8
- ✓ Luke 20:34
- ✓ Romans 12:2
- ✓ 1 Corinthians 1:20
- ✓ 1 Corinthians 2:6-8
- ✓ 1 Corinthians 3:18
- ✓ 2 Corinthians 4:4 (The Adversary is "the god of this eon")
- ✓ Galatians 1:3-5 ("the present wicked eon")
- ✓ 1 Timothy 6:17
- ✓ 2 Timothy 4:9-10
- ✓ Titus 2:11-13
- ✓ Ephesians 2:2 ("In accord with the eon of this world")

JESUS REFERRED TO THE END OF THE PRESENT EON *(Singular)*
- ✓ Matthew 13:39
- ✓ Matthew 13:49
- ✓ Matthew 24:3
- ✓ Matthew 28:20

THE IMPENDING, OR COMING EON
(If "the eon" is endless, what is meant by "the impending eon?")
- ✓ Mark 10:30
- ✓ Luke 18:30
- ✓ Hebrews 6:5

MULTIPLE EONS REFERENCED
- ✓ Matthew 12:32 ("Neither in this eon nor in that which is impending")
- ✓ Luke 20:35 ("This eon" is compared with "that eon")
- ✓ Jude 1:25 ("for all the eons")
- ✓ Ephesians 1:21 ("Not only in this eon, but also in that which is impending")
- ✓ Ephesians 2:7 ("the oncoming eons") – plural

(Note: Besides the present eon there are at least two eons to come, noting the reference to "the oncoming eons" in Ephesians 2:7.)

REFERENCE TO THE CONCLUSION OF THE EONS *(Plural)*

Hebrews 9:26 speaks of Christ's sacrifice, and notes that "at the conclusion of the eons" He is manifest for the repudiation of sin through His sacrifice. While His sacrifice has taken place long ago, and while many in this present age have been reconciled through His work upon the cross, at the end of the eons He will be manifest that the fullness of His work will be accomplished. We see this happening in 1 Corinthians 15:20-28.

ONE EON COMPARED TO OTHER EONS
    ✓ "The eon of the eons" (Ephesians 3:21)

AN EON THAT FOLLOWS THE PREVIOUS EON
    ✓ "The eon of the eon" (Hebrews 1:8)

MULTIPLE EONS COMPARED WITH ALL OF THE EONS
(*"Eons of the eons" appears in the following passages.*)
    ✓ Romans 16:27
    ✓ Galatians 1:5
    ✓ Philippians 4:20
    ✓ 1 Timothy 1:17
    ✓ 2 Timothy 4:18
    ✓ Hebrews 13:21
    ✓ 1 Peter 4:11
    ✓ 1 Peter 5:11
    ✓ Revelation 1:6,18
    ✓ Revelation 4:9,10
    ✓ Revelation 5:13
    ✓ Revelation 7:12
    ✓ Revelation 10:6
    ✓ Revelation 11:15
    ✓ Revelation 14:11
    ✓ Revelation 15:7
    ✓ Revelation 19:3
    ✓ Revelation 20:10
    ✓ Revelation 22:5

EONIAN
Since there are multiple periods of time referred to as eons ("aion" in the Greek), each with a beginning and an end, it would follow that the adjective "eonian" would carry the meaning "for an eon" or "for the eons." But while something may last "for the eons" this cannot carry the

meaning "forever" or "endless," since eons are peiods of time that have a conclusion.

PURPOSE OF THE EONS
- ✓ Ephesians 3:9-11 ("in accord with the purpose of the eons")

WE GET A GLIMPSE OF THIS PURPOSE IN THE FOLLOWING:
- ✓ Ephesians 1:8-11 ("to head up all in the Christ ... operating all in accord with the counsel of His will")
- ✓ Philippians 2:9-11 ("every knee should be bowing, celestial and terrestrial and subterranean...")
- ✓ Colossians 1:15-21 ("and thru Him (Christ) to reconcile all to Him...")
- ✓ 1 Corinthians 15:28 (God becoming "All in all")

LIKELY PROGRESSION OF THE EONS (Hypothesis)
- ✓ [Before the eons]
- ✓ 1 – Creation to disruption (Genesis 1:2)
- ✓ 2 – Disruption to Flood
- ✓ 3 – Flood to Christ's return
- ✓ 4 – Christ's return to Great White Throne
- ✓ 5 – Great White Throne to Consummation
- ✓ [After the eons]

Eon	eons	before the eons	end of the eon
End of the eons	eon of the eon	eon of the eons	eons of the eons

The eons (Greek "aion")

Before the eons (1 Corinthians 2:6-8)   All is out of God (1 Corinthians 8:6)
Before times eonian (Titus 1:1-3; 2 Timothy 1:9-10)

Creation   EON #1
This is the "then world" that perished (2 Peter 3:6)

God created the heavens and the earth (Genesis 1:1)   Not created as chaos (Isaiah 45:18)
The earth <u>became</u> a chaos and vacant (Genesis 1:2)   The "disruption" (Ephesians 1:3-4)

Order   EON #2
This is the "ancient world" (2 Peter 2:5)

Creation of man (Genesis 2)   Disobedience
Mankind grows in number   Evil is great (Genesis 6:5)
God floods the earth

Age of Promise   EON #3
This is the "present wicked eon" (Galatians 1:4)

Man commanded to fill the earth (Gen 9:1)   God scatters man (Gen 11:8)
Promise to bless all thru Abraham (Gen 12:3)   Abraham believes – righteousness (15:6)
Promise passes to Isaac (Genesis 26:2)   To Jacob/Israel (Genesis 28:13)
God gives the Law thru Moses   Kingdom established thru David/Solomon
Exile   Prophets promise restoration of kingdom
Kingdom proclaimed as near (John Baptist)   John persecuted
Kingdom proclaimed as near (Jesus)   Jesus crucified
Kingdom proclaimed as near (Peter)   Kingdom evangel rejected

<< *Israel set aside*   *Paul's evangel to Jew/Gentile equally* >>
<< *Body of Christ*   *Body of Christ to be "snatched away"* >>

Tribulation upon the earth (Revelation)   God working thru Israel (Revelation)

Christ Returns to Reign   EON #4
This is "coming eon" (Mark 10:30)

Christ reigns on David's throne   Judgment
Destruction of the earth (2 Peter 3:10)

New heavens & earth   EON #5
A "new heavens and a new earth in which righteousness
is dwelling (2 Peter 3:13)

Christ reigns <u>until</u> all enemies under His feet (1 Corinthians 15:25)
Last enemy (death) defeated (1 Corinthians 15:27)
The consummation (1 Corinthians 15:24)

God All in all (1 Corinthians 15:28)

Evangel

The Greek *evangel* is most always translated *gospel* in our Bible versions, except in cases where our notion of *gospel* does not fit. We place great faith in the translator, and in orthodox teachings, when we use our English Bibles to understand what the *gospel* is. The fact is that *evangel* simply means *good news;* nothing more.

We tend to think there is a single *gospel* for all eras, and when we hear the word we immediately conjure the notion of "the gospel" that has indoctrinated us. But the good news can, and does, differ from one context to another. In 1 Thessalonians 3:6 for example, *evangel* simply refers to the good news that Paul received concerning the faith of the Thessalonian believers. In Matthew we see it is *the evangel of the kingdom* that is being proclaimed. If we study carefully we will note that this evangel is much different from what Paul later proclaimed to the Gentiles, who have their expectation in *the celestial realm* and not in the kingdom to come upon the earth.

Whenever we see the word *evangel* (or *gospel* in most English versions) we should always ask ourselves what the good news consists of in that specific context. The Concordant Version simply uses the transliteration *evangel* instead of the word *gospel* so that our thinking will not be biased by any preconceived notions.

Gospel

See "Evangel"

Healing

There is a strong relationship between teaching, heralding, and healing during Jesus' earthly ministry. But as we observe God's works in a particular era we cannot assume He will work in the same way in all eras. During His ministry Jesus was proclaiming the evangel of the kingdom. This message pertains only to Israel. When Paul is later commissioned to proclaim a different evangel to a different group, we will see a decline of visible signs. Consider this. Timothy suffered *often infirmities*. (1 Timothy 5:23) There was no prayer for healing; he was prescribed wine. Epaphroditus was sick and close to death, yet Paul did not attempt to heal him. He even left Trophimus at Miletum sick. Why did Paul not pray for his healing?

Today the Body of Christ has its expectation in the celestial realm, not in this earthly realm. We have no expectation of a physical land. We await the Lord to snatch us away into the heavens, (1 Thessalonians 4:13ff) not to come and establish the kingdom here upon the earth. That is Israel's expectation. It would make sense that a message concerning things to occur upon the earth would be accompanied by signs such as healing that have an effect in life upon the earth. This is not to say that God will no longer bring supernatural healing in some instances. But the relationship we see in Matthew between teaching, heralding and healing is no longer the same today as we proclaim the evangel of peace, reconciliation and grace that has been charged to us in this present era.

Heaven

Sometimes the word heaven, or heavens, speaks of the atmosphere directly above the earth. Other times it speaks of somewhere well beyond, but its precise location is not revealed.

Paradise is not heaven. As a matter of fact, Paradise is the Persian word for park, and it simply refers to the conditions upon the earth when the kingdom is restored unto Israel. It will be a recapturing of the Garden of Eden, also a place upon the earth.

A.E. Knoch defines *heaven* as "what is seen when looking up. In the singular it seems to be confined to the sky or gaseous envelope of the earth (Matthew 16:1). In the plural it includes the entire universe except the earth (Genesis 1:1; Colossians 1:16)."

The Israelites never had any thoughts of "going to heaven." Their hope and expectation was the coming of the Messiah to establish His kingdom upon the earth. This is what Jesus speaks of during His earthly ministry. After His resurrection, when the apostles asked if this was the time He intended to restore the kingdom unto Israel, He did not tell them they had it all wrong. He simply said it was not theirs to know God's timing. (Acts 1:6-7) Israel is God's instrument upon the earth. When He returns, born-again Israel will serve a purpose in Christ's reign. Today Israel, which rejected the Messiah, is temporarily set aside as Christ now draws those of the nations into the Body of Christ. But the "stubbornness" in Israel is temporary. (Romans 11:25-26) When the events described in Revelation take place, Israel will once again play a part.

Paul speaks of things not previously revealed, and one of those things is "heaven." Those of Israel look for Christ to come to earth where their expectation lies in the ages to come. We within the Body of Christ look for Christ to come and snatch us away to be with Him, where we will play a part in the heavens in the ages to come.

There are few details about "heaven" provided in the Bible. The notion of pearly gates and St. Peter admitting us are non-Biblical notions, not based on the Scriptures. The images we see in Revelation pertain to the earth; either this present earth or the new earth. The New Jerusalem with all of its splendor comes down out of heaven, but is not heaven itself.

Who goes to heaven? The Body of Christ (believers) will be called up to meet the Lord in the air, and we will serve the Lord in the heavens. When all things are reconciled to God and He becomes All in all, (1 Corinthians 15:28) the entire universe will be under the realm of God's kingdom.

It has not been revealed to us exactly what this will look like; who will be in heaven and who will be upon the new earth. But we know that the heavens are superior to the earth. Isaiah 55:9 tells us that the heavens are loftier than the earth. Nehemiah 9:6 tells us the heavens are inhabited. But without further details being provided we will simply need to trust God as to the place He has planned for each of us. But He is our Heavenly Father, filled with grace and love, and most certainly we can trust Him for specifically what lies ahead!

Hell

When we see this word in an English translation it comes from one of three Greek words; *Hades, Gehenna* or *Tartarus.*

Hades simply means *unseen.* It is the temporary destination for everyone when they die, righteous and wicked alike. The flesh returns to the soil, the spirit returns to God, and the soul goes to *the unseen place* (hades). The Hebrew *sheol* in the Old Testament is the equivalent to *hades* in the Greek. Bible translators have tainted the pure Word of God with their opinions and theologies. When they find hades or sheol with reference to one who is wicked, they translate it "hell." But when they find the same word with reference to one who is righteous, they translate it "grave" or "death." If we look at hades and sheol in every instance in the Scriptures, we will see it simply refers to the unseen place where the soul goes immediately upon death.

The Greek *gehenna* is first mentioned in Matthew 5:22. It is the Greek form of the Hebrew *Gai Hinnom* or *Valley of Hinnom;* a ravine just below Jerusalem. This place is referred to in 2 Chronicles 28:3 and 33:6. In

Jesus' day it was a refuse dump with fires perpetually burning. When Jesus talked about *Gehenna* his audience understood that He referred to the refuse dump outside of Jerusalem. For certain crimes once the kingdom is restored, the bodies of the guilty will be cast into this place; a disgraceful fate. Isaiah 66:22-24 foretells of this place, and the terminology used shows that it is clearly a physical, geographic location. *All flesh* will see the corpses of the *mortals* burning in the fire as they come to Jerusalem to worship. As Jesus spoke, this was His first reference to Gehenna. Had He been referring to a spiritual place of endless torment, something different from this *Valley of Hinnom* that the Jews were familiar with, this would have been a new concept and many questions would have been asked and clarifications needed. From Genesis forward the penalty for sin is death, not endless torment. If Jesus is changing the penalty to endless torment, certainly He would have provided further explanation as to this change.

Tartarus is a place where wicked spirits (demons) are imprisoned. No person is ever said to be cast into Tartarus.

Holy

If we examine the word *holy* or *hallowed* throughout the Bible we will see that its meaning is to be *set apart* or *differentiated*. God is holy (*set apart*), and He designates certain people or things as holy; not because they have any special merit but <u>because God has chosen them</u> to be used in some fashion for his purposes. The clothing to be used by the priests in the Old Testament was not inherently *better* than other clothing, and the animals deemed to be *clean* were not inherently *better* or more righteous than other animals. God created them all. But God chose certain clothing and certain animals to be *set apart;* to *differentiate* his people from other peoples of the earth. And when one is designated *holy*, God defines certain behaviors for that individual that are acceptable, and that differentiate that one from others.

So holy does not mean better or more righteous than others. Holy simply means *set apart* or *differentiated* from others. In the Old Testament God delivered to Israel (His set apart people) the Law; but Israel found it impossible to keep the Law. As it turns out the Law was used to show the people their helplessness to be righteous based on their works, and it led them to Christ. In Galatians, Paul would tell the believers that they were freed from the Law. The elements of the Law were no longer requirements for God's people, although Paul continues to encourage the believers to live a life that was worthy of God's grace that had been given to them freely. So in the Old Testament, God's people (Israel) were set apart, and they were expected to follow very detailed set-apart behaviors to be righteous. In the present era, through God's grace the set-apart people (Body of Christ) are *holy* regardless of behavior. Certain behavior is described as acceptable and other behavior as unacceptable, but regardless of behavior those within the Body of Christ are saved and continue to be God's holy people.

Kingdom

We must always examine the context to understand the aspect of God's kingdom that is being referred to. The kingdom is in full force in the heavens, but not yet upon the earth. Hence the prayer, *Thy kingdom come, Thy will be done, on earth as it is in heaven.*

Paul's reference to *His celestial kingdom* (2 Timothy 4:18) refers to the kingdom already realized in the celestials, or the heavens. But the many references Jesus makes to the kingdom in Matthew, for example, refer to the time when God's kingdom will become a reality upon the earth. Yes, in some aspects the kingdom is already in place within the believer (the kingdom is within you). But in the fullest sense, the kingdom to come upon the earth will be realized once Christ physically returns and reigns (as we see in Revelation).

We remember that David's kingdom was ordained by God and established upon the earth. Later the prophets proclaimed that there would be a restoration of this kingdom unto Israel with a successor king from David's lineage. Daniel foretold that this would be greater than all other kingdoms.

Many today believe these references to the kingdom are not talking of a return of the *physical* kingdom upon the earth, but are instead *figurative* references. But certainly the disciples were expecting a physical kingdom to come upon the earth after the resurrection (Acts 1:6) and Jesus does not tell them they have misunderstood. He simply tells them it is not theirs to know the timing of certain things that will take place. In Revelation we see Christ's return to the earth and the establishment of the kingdom in the eon that follows this present eon. Even in the final eon (Revelation 21:1) when John perceives *a new heaven and a new earth* and sees *the holy city, new Jerusalem, descending out of heaven;* we note that it <u>descends out of heaven</u>. The city is not heaven itself!

Throughout Revelation, as the kingdom upon the earth becomes a reality, we note the distinct Jewish character. The twelve tribes (Revelation 21:12) and twelve apostles (Revelation 21:14) are prominent. The nations are not found within the city, but are outside. (Revelation 21:24) How different this is from Paul's description of the heavenly realm with no barrier between Jew and Gentile. In Revelation the leaves on the tree are *for the cure of the nations*, (Revelation 22:2) implying physical bodies in need of the leaves to sustain life. Compare this with the incorruptible spiritual body described by Paul. (1 Corinthians 15:42) When we hear of the lake of fire burning (Revelation 21:8) it is further described as the *second death*. But Paul tells us *the last enemy is being abolished: death.* (1 Corinthians 15:27) When we see Christ reigning upon the throne (Revelation 21:5) as promised by the prophets of old we think of Paul's words, that Christ must reign UNTIL He places all enemies under His feet, and then when all is subject to Christ He subjects Himself to God Who becomes All in all. (1 Corinthians 15:25,28) And when we hear that the slaves of God are reigning, (Revelation 22:5) and that there are *kings of the earth*, (Revelation 21:24) we think of Paul's proclamation that all sovereignty, authority and power are nullified. (1 Corinthians 15:24)

Revelation describes the kingdom of heaven coming upon the earth, with Christ reigning. This is the kingdom John the Baptist and Jesus are announcing in Matthew. But the king, and therefore the kingdom, are rejected by the Jews. During this time in which we now live, while Israel is temporarily set aside, salvation is given to the Gentiles. (Romans 11:25) When God is ready, the kingdom will come upon the earth, although it is not ours to know the timing. (Acts 1:7) And when God is ready, when at last every knee is bowing and all are subjected to Him, the final eon will come to its conclusion. (1 Corinthians 15) Death (the lake of fire) will be abolished, all will have found salvation through the grace of God and the work of Christ upon the cross, and God will be All in all.

Lake of Fire

This comes the closest to the common notions concerning hell, with two primary differences. First, the lake of fire does not last "forever and ever," but only for the eons of the eons (several eons, which we recall are periods of time with a beginning and an end). Second, the purpose of the lake of fire is not to torture and torment but to bring about a positive conclusion in accord with God's plans.

Matthew may be alluding to the lake of fire when he tells of the judgment to come when Christ returns and judges those living upon the earth based upon their works. (Matthew 25:31-46) In verse 46, those who do not pass the test are not cast into eternal torment but will experience "eonian chastening." Even the well-respected William Barclay indicated that the Greek words used in this instance are never used to imply destruction, but constructive chastening.

Revelation 20:15 tells us what the lake of fire is; *the second death*. And in 1 Corinthians 15:27 we see that as all things are brought into subjection to Christ, the last enemy (death) is abolished. So, there is a conclusion to the lake of fire.

Pardon

We observe in the parable of the unmerciful servant (Matthew 18:23) that pardon can be revoked. In the parable it is contingent on the recipient granting pardon to others. Pardon is something a king (executive) has authority to grant. Justification, on the other hand, is something a judge (judicial) has the authority to grant. Pardon recognizes that the individual is guilty but the sentence is suspended. Justification (which Paul speaks of frequently) recognizes the individual is innocent.

In the kingdom age (see Matthew) we see pardon being offered. But Paul speaks of justification, not pardon. Let us pay close attention to details like this, and not assume that things like pardon and justification are the same thing. Similarly, we should pay close attention to the distinctions between such things as born again vs. new creation, kingdom of God vs. the heavenlies, and the evangel of the kingdom vs. the evangel of grace.

Resurrection (the expectation of various groups)

There are numerous passages that refer to the resurrection of various groups of people at different times.

Resurrection event #1 (1 Thessalonians 4:13-18): The dead in Christ will be raised, along with those in Christ who are alive, when "the rapture" occurs. This event is not revealed elsewhere in the Scriptures but only by Paul who was given the gospel of the Uncircumcision. (Galatians 2:7-9) Paul writes that those in Christ will be *snatched away* to meet the Lord in the air. This is a different event from when Christ returns to the earth to reign. Israel awaits His return to the earth to restore the kingdom unto Israel. (Acts 1:6-7) But the Body of Christ awaits Him to snatch us away to meet Him in the air. Israel's expectation is to serve God upon the earth when Christ reigns. Our expectation is to serve Him in the celestials (the heavens) where we will be a display of His grace in the oncoming eons. (Ephesians 2:6-7)

After this resurrection of the Body of Christ, the time of God's indignation (The Great Tribulation) as foretold in the book of Revelation will occur. Note that the Body of Christ is to be rescued out of the coming indignation. (1 Thessalonians 1:10) God did not appoint us to indignation. (1 Thessalonians 5:8-9) At the conclusion of this time of Tribulation, Christ will return to the earth. (Revelation 19:11ff) Thrones will be setup and there will be a judgment of those living at the time of Christ's return. (Revelation 20:4; Matthew 25:31)

Resurrection event #2 (Revelation 20:4-5): The passage tells us this is "the former resurrection." Those who have been executed because of the testimony of Jesus and because of the word of God, and who do not worship the wild beast or its image, and who did not take the emblem (mark) of the beast will be resurrected. These will live and reign with Christ a thousand years. (Revelation 20:5) While the Body of Christ is reigning in service to God in the heavens, the group described here from among Israel will reign in service to God upon the earth.

After the thousand year reign, Satan will be loosed (Revelation 20:7) and will deceive the nations, mobilizing them for battle. The Adversary (Satan) will be cast into the lake of fire to be tormented for the eons of the eons (at least two eons, out of all the eons).

Resurrection event #3 (Revelation 20:11-15): The sea and hades give up their dead. They are resurrected and stand before the throne and are judged in accord with their acts. Those not found in the scroll of life are cast into the lake of fire. (Note that the duration of their time in the lake of fire; the second death; is not mentioned as it was for the Adversary.)

Then we see this present heaven and earth coming to an end and the creation of a new heaven and a new earth. (Revelation 21:1) Sometime after this, when all are subjected to God, will come the "consummation." (1 Corinthians 15:20-28) This is the climax of history. As in Adam all are dying, so also in Christ are all made alive. Christ reigns until all enemies are under His feet (subjected to Him), and the last enemy (death) is abolished. Christ is then subjected to God the Father, as God becomes All in all.

If the lake of fire is a *figurative* death there is no need for a subsequent resurrection event, as all have previously been resurrected. And once the lake of fire has accomplished its purpose of bringing its inhabitants into subjection, it is eliminated. If the lake of fire is a second, *literal* death, there must be an implied resurrection of all those that were cast in; if all are to ultimately become subjected and reconciled to God (as the Scriptures indicate) and if God is to become All in all.

Rightly dividing the Scriptures

Paul made it very clear to Timothy that it was necessary to "rightly divide" the Word of God to understand how all parts of the Bible fit together.

"Endeavor to present yourself to God qualified, an unashamed worker, correctly cutting the word of truth." (2 Timothy 2:15)

In other words; all parts of Scripture were not directed to all of mankind in all eras. Some parts were directed specifically to Israel, for example, and those portions cannot be "stolen" by those outside of Israel. Attempts to apply ALL parts of the Bible to ALL people-groups and ALL eras has brought much distortion, confusion, and error to that which God has revealed in His Word. It is one thing to KNOW what God's Word says; to memorize it or to become intimately familiar with Bible passages. But it is another, and far more important thing, to understand how all of God's Word fits together, for only then will we understand its meaning and application to our lives.

God's Word is progressive and unfolding. God began with creation, and selected certain individuals thru whom He would speak ... Abraham, Isaac, Jacob (Israel), and then the people of Israel. So God moved from working thru select individuals to working thru an entire nation; Israel. But even then, it was His intent to bless all the peoples of the earth; all nations; thru Israel. (See Genesis 12:3; 22:18; 26:4-5; 28:14)

When Israel began to go astray God chose prophets to speak to the nation and to call her back to repentance and obedience. But continued rebellion led to exile. Still the prophets spoke and promised a restoration of the kingdom that had once been established by David. The people awaited this restoration and the promised Messiah who would bring the restoration.

In the gospel accounts the Messiah (Christ) comes, speaking of the nearness of the kingdom. This was the promise the people had been waiting for. But Christ was rejected by Israel, and as a result there was a delay in the kingdom's restoration. But in Acts the Twelve carry on with the same message. If the people would repent, Christ would return and there would be a restoration of the kingdom. (Acts 3:19-21) But still the people rejected Christ (Acts 28:26-28), and the kingdom was further delayed.

So God did a new thing; an amazing thing. Setting aside Israel temporarily He spoke directly to the nations thru a new apostle; Paul. Paul was not one of the Twelve, but was an ADDITIONAL apostle with a new mission, unheard of in the past. He would speak to the nations, introducing the Body of Christ consisting of Jew and Gentile alike with no barrier or preference. This created no small stir, for Israel was offended by this heretical message. (Acts 22:21-23) THEY were the people of God, not the nations.

While Paul proclaimed the message assigned to him (the evangel of the Uncircumcision per Galatians 2:7), Peter and the others continued with their message to Israel ... repent and the kingdom would be restored. Peter and the other Circumcision writers penned their letters to the Circumcision as they awaited the kingdom. Repent, have faith and good works, and persevere! Israel still awaited the kingdom. And Revelation is the fulfillment of what they waited for. Christ, the King, returns; the kingdom is established once again; and faithful Israel serves its place as Christ rules over all the nations.

But what happened to the Body of Christ? Israel is mentioned time and again throughout Revelation, but whenever the nations are mentioned it is always negative. It is Israel as contrasted with the nations. Nowhere do we see "the church" or the Body of Christ. This shows us that somewhere along the way the Body of Christ was removed from the scene in order that the turbulent times could proceed, and Satan could lead the ultimate rebellion without being impeded by the Body of Christ or the holy spirit that filled them. We see this "removal" in 1 Thessalonians 4 when Christ sounds the trump, the dead in Christ rise, and the living in Christ rise to meet Him in the air. And the Body of Christ begins its commission of reigning in the heavens, for its expectation was always related to the celestials and not the earth. And then, sometime after this, Christ returns to the earth and restores the kingdom with faithful Israel reigning with Him.

The Body of Christ reigning in the heavens, and Israel reigning upon the earth, we see the final phase of God's restoration process taking place. All of life to this point has been a process, but now we get closer and closer to the final goal. Paul records this in 1 Corinthians 15 where we see death abolished, all subjected to Christ, and God becoming All in all.

While Revelation may be positioned as the final book in the Bible, it does not reveal to us the "final condition" of mankind. At the end of the book the process continues, and only in Paul's writings are we told of the conclusion; the consummation.

Today we live in an era of grace as revealed to us by the apostle Paul. God is conciliated to the world, not reckoning mankind's offenses to them. (2 Corinthians 5:19) But a day will come when God will take the next step in His plan to reconcile all to Himself. Grace will not reign in that future era, but judgment; for judgment is what it will take to bring the most stubborn and rebellious into the fold.

In that future era Christ's ambassadors (2 Corinthians 5:20) will be recalled, as is typically the case when conditions become perilous in the nations where ambassadors serve. War is about to be declared on the rebellious world.

Even today mankind seems to have not only forgotten God, but has lost all consciousness to His existence. He is shut out of their every thought. And in the future era described in Revelation, this will be true to the extreme!

Sabbath(s)

The word *sabbath* does not signify rest, though it is often translated such in Bible translations. God did not need to rest. Rather, he *ceased*. Man needs to cease from his efforts and his vain attempts to keep the law to earn righteousness, thereby saving himself. The *sabbath* was intended to show the futility in doing so, and the need for dependence upon God alone.

We tend to think of the *Sabbath* as a weekly occurrence (Saturday). But Leviticus 23 summarizes seven festivals/feasts that are referred to as *special Sabbaths*. Some Sabbaths occur in close proximity. For example, on the tenth day of the seventh month we have the Day of Covering (Atonement) and five days later is another Sabbath; the Festival of Ingathering. The *evening of the Sabbaths* is where an evening ends one Sabbath and begins another. Occasionally a festival falls on the weekly Sabbath, in which case we have a double Sabbath, or *the day of the Sabbaths*. When we see the phrase *one of the Sabbaths* it refers to the series of Sabbaths between Wave Sheaf and Pentecost.

In Matthew 28:1 Mary Magdalene and the other Mary come to the sepulcher at the lighting up into *one of the Sabbaths. One of the Sabbaths* is often erroneously translated the *first day of the week*, giving the notion that the resurrection occurred on Sunday. There is no linguistic warrant to render the translation in this way; it is only carelessness and the contamination of the Scriptures by religious tradition. There is no word in the Greek for first, or day, or week found anywhere in this passage. In Matthew 28:1 we have just concluded Passover a few days earlier, and *one of the Sabbaths* would refer to the regular weekly Sabbath; a Saturday.

Salvation / Saved

This is an interesting word. If you were raised in the church, you'll immediately think you know what "saved" means ... that you are saved from eternal torment. But saved NEVER means saved from eternal torment, as the doctrine of eternal torment is a fabrication of man's teachings and is not found in God's Word.

The word saved is used many times in the Bible. Generally it means to be saved from death. One's life might be saved from being killed by an enemy. It sometimes means saved from disease (equivalent to being healed). Often in the New Testament it means saved from the indignation, wrath or tribulation that we read about in Revelation.

Whenever we encounter the word *saved* we should seek from the context to understand, "Saved from what?" The believer in this present age is saved from God's indignation that will come upon the earth following "the rapture." (1 Thessalonians 4:13ff) But it is important to remember that ultimately all will be saved from death, indignation, tribulation, etc. For it is God's will that *all* mankind be saved, (1 Timothy 2:4) and God is operating *all* in accord with the counsel of His will. (Ephesians 1:11) We see this occurring at the climax of history when God becomes All in all. (1 Corinthians 15:28)

Sin / Transgression

A *transgression* is the willful breaking of a known law or instruction; the violation of a rule. A *sin* is, literally, missing the mark. It is a failure to measure up to the standard.

Soul

The soul is the consciousness aspect of man. It is what gives us sensation. The soul is generated when the body (from the soil) and spirit (from God) are joined, much as light is produced when a filament is animated by "life-giving" electricity. When God's spirit animated the soil, Adam was given life.

At death the body (soil) returns to the soil, the spirit returns to God, and the soul goes to *hades* (literally *the unseen*.) There is no consciousness.

There is no life. This is true for all men, including both the righteous and the wicked.

What is the meaning of having one's soul saved? This could refer to enjoying conscious life in this present age (the life we currently experience), but most often in the Scriptures it refers to having conscious life in the age to come. Those whose souls have been saved will enjoy conscious life in the age to come after they are resurrected, while those not saved will not. But in either case, *all* will ultimately experience life, for God is the Saviour of all, and this will be fully realized at the consummation when God becomes All in all. (1 Corinthians 15:28)

What is the difference between killing the body and killing the soul? (Matthew 10:28) At the resurrection, in the next eon, the soul will live again. Those in Christ will enjoy eonian life, but those not in Christ will remain in the unseen place. One need not fear a man who can kill only the body, for the soul will re-appear in the next eon at the resurrection. (1 Thessalonians 4:13ff) Instead one should fear God, Who is able to destroy the body <u>and</u> keep the soul in hades, thereby forfeiting life in the eon to come. But despite this, God will ultimately restore all mankind once the eons have concluded. (1 Corinthians 15)

Works, Rewards for

Those still living upon the earth when Christ returns will be gathered and judged based upon their works. (Matthew 25:31-46) The "sheep" are given life eonian (25:46) in the kingdom (25:34) where Christ will now reign upon the earth. The "goats" will be cast into the *fire eonian* (25:41) for eonian *chastening.* (25:46)

The deceased non-believer will be judged *in accord with their acts* by Christ after His return to the earth at the great white throne. (Revelation 20:12) Those not found written in the scroll of life will be cast into the lake of fire. (20:15)

Note that the eonian chastening is not an eternal condition; but is *eonian* (for the eon or eons). Even the lake of fire, also referred to as the second death (Revelation 21:8) will one day be *abolished,* (1 Corinthians 15:27) when all are finally subjected to God and He becomes All in all. For just as every creature is created in Him (Christ) and through Him ... so also through Him will all be reconciled. (Colossians 1:15-20)

Today the believer is saved by grace apart from works, so there are no grounds for boasting. (Romans 3:21-28) But the believer should beware as to how he builds upon the foundation with works. (1 Corinthians 3:10-15) Those believers who exhibit worthwhile works will get *wages*. (3:14) Those with works that are not worthwhile will still be saved, yet as through fire. (3:15) Each believer will give account for his actions at the dais of God. (Romans 14:10-13) At the dais each will be *requited* (paid) for that which he puts into practice through the body, whether good or bad. (2 Corinthians 5:10)

Worship

The Greek word translated *worship* is *proskuneo*, which literally means "toward-teem." Our notion of what worship consists of has been shaped by the religious traditions and ideas of men. To determine the true meaning of worship as used in the Scriptures we should examine every instance where the word is used. Using the Keyword Concordance which is contained within the Concordant Literal New Testament, we can study every occurrence of *proskuneo*.

In Matthew 15:6 we see that the Canaanite woman *coming, worships Him.* We learn from this instance that worship does not always occur within a group setting. And it is not always done thru singing as some today believe. If we examine every occurrence of the word in the New Testament, we see that worship is simply a coming near, a reverence for, and a faith in the object of worship ... whatever outward shape this may take. Let the reader search every occurrence of *proskuneo* to see what the Lord has revealed concerning worship.

A Word about Bible Translations

Today there are many different Bible translations to choose from. Some of the newer ones have been written (in my opinion) for financial gain; to sell Bibles. And those written with the intent to provide an easy-to-read translation incorporate the translators' opinions and theologies into the translation, making them *interpretations* instead of pure translations. Many different Hebrew or Greek words are often translated using a single English word, making it impossible to recognize distinctions without using laborious study helps. The translators have done this because they have determined there is no practical difference between certain Hebrew and Greek words; but what if they are wrong? Similarly, a single word in the Hebrew or Greek is often translated using different English words with drastically different meanings. Here the translators assume to know that God was using a single word to refer to very different ideas. Could the translators be wrong in their assumptions?

In his "Proponents for a Literal Translation of the New Testament," Frank Neil Pohorlak writes: "The Word of God is revealed by means of words. If the words we use to translate the Word conceal rather than reveal, then the thoughts of God cannot be known or acted upon." A PRECISE translation is needed to properly reveal God's message; not a translation that is dumbed-down and easy to read, where the translator has made many judgment calls along the way.

I appreciate the Concordant Version, not because I trust the translators more than other translators, but because of the methodology used. Great care was taken to allow the reader to distinguish between different Greek or Hebrew words. Whenever possible, an English word is only used for a single Greek or Hebrew word, and each Hebrew or Greek word is translated using the same consistent English word or idea. Meanings of words are derived by using a concordance to examine every instance where a word is used in Scripture.

There is a keyword concordance in the back of the New Testament that allows the reader to look at all other instances where the same Greek word was used, thereby checking the translation. This methodology may make the translation more difficult to read, but it also preserves the distinctions made in God's Word in the original languages, and it prevents the bias of the translator from creeping into the translation as much as is humanly possible.

Grace & Truth Magazine, Volume 65 has this to say in the Editorial: "Though scarcely noted in religious circles – except by an enlightened few – we have no hesitation in claiming this [Concordant] version to be a great step forward in the presentation of God's Word. Many sincere folks, when reading Scripture, are unaware they are reading a translation filtered to a greater or lesser extent through the mind of the translator. The Concordant method, pioneered by the late A. E. Knoch, to a great extent prevents opinion and bias from influencing the translation. ...

[Concerning the Concordant Version of the Old Testament] A. E. Knoch stressed that no human work could ever be perfect, but we have no hesitation in saying we know of no other version that achieves the accuracy of the C. V. It brings the reader closer to the inspired original text and enlightens the mind to the Hebrew idioms in a way not found in other versions. We heartily recommend it to you."

The Concordant Version can be ordered from *The Concordant Publishing Concern* at concordant.org Grace & Truth Magazine can be contacted at gracetruth.co.uk

Concordance of Key Passages

ALL
Savior of *all,* especially believers (1 Tim 4:10 – see Gal 6:10 for context)
God wills that *all* mankind be saved (1 Tim 2:4)
Operating *all* in accord with counsel of His will (Eph 1:11)
Correspondent ransom for *all* – testimony in its own eras (1 Tim 2:6)
In Adam *all* dying; in Christ *all* vivified (1 Cor 15:21-23)
One offense for *all* mankind for condemnation... (Rom 5:18-19)
Lamb of God taking away sin of *the world* (John 1:29)
Every knee bowing (Phil 2:9-11; Is 45:23)
Locks *all* in stubbornness; to be merciful to *all* (Rom 11:30-32)
All created ... to reconcile *all* (Col 1:16-20)
He should be tasting death for the sake of *everyone* (Heb 2:9)
God was in Christ conciliating *the world* to Himself (2 Cor 5:19)
For our sins, not ours only but *the whole world* (1 John 2:2)
For all, and *on* all who are believing (Romans 3:22)
Son of man came to seek and to save the "destroyed" (Luke 19:10)
Shall be drawing all to Myself (John 12:32)
All people blessed (Gen 12:3; 22:18; 26:5; 28:14)

BEHAVIOR
Walk worthily (Eph 4:1)
Working for the good of all (Gal 6:10)
Put on (behavior) ... over all love (Col 3:12-17)
Be gentle toward all (2 Tim 2:22-26)
The dais (Rom 14:10; 2 Cor 5:10)

BELIEF
Reckoned as righteousness (Rom 4:3)
None seeking God (Rom 3:10-11)
Belief on Christ graciously granted by God (Phil 1:29)
Apprehensions of unbelievers blinded by god of this eon (2 Cor 4:3)
Lydia's heart opened (Acts 16:13)
Systematizing deception (Eph 4:14)
Doubting Thomas (John 20:24-29)

BODY OF CHRIST: CHRIST'S COMPLEMENT. SONS OF GOD
His body ... the complement of the One completing the all in all (Eph 1:23)
The complement of Christ (Eph 4:14)
Peacemakers shall be called sons of God (Matt 5:9)
Men after the resurrection are "sons of God" (Luke 20:36)
Those led by God's spirit are sons of God (Rom 8;14)
You are all sons of God, thru faith in Christ Jesus (Gal 3:26)

CHRIST'S COMMISSION TO ISRAEL
Twelve to go to lost sheep of Israel (Matt 10:6)
Won't finish cities of Israel before Son of Man comes (Matt 10:23)

CHRIST AS TO-SUBJECTOR
Christ bringing all into subjection (1 Cor 15:25-28)
Making known secret of His will, to head up all in the Christ (Eph 1:9)
The One completing the all in all (Eph 1:23)
Thru Him to reconcile all to Him (Col 1:20)

DEATH
Only Christ immortal (1 Tim 6:16)
Mortal must put on immortality (1 Cor 15:53)
Soil returns to soil (Ecc 12:7)
Dead know nothing (Ecc 9:5)
No one remembers you when he is dead (Ps 6:5)
Multitudes who sleep will awake (Dan 12:2)

ECCLESIA (ORGANIZATION)
At the house of Prisca & Aquila (Rom 16:5; 1 Cor 16:19)
If the whole ecclesia should come together (1 Cor 14:23)
Coming together not for the better (1 Cor 11:17)

ECCLESIA (PURPOSE)
Life eonian a gracious gift (Rom 6:23)
Sealed w holy spirit ... earnest of allotment (Eph 1:13-14)
Eonian life = real life (Phil 3:4-13; 1 Tim 6:12,19)
Joint enjoyers of Christ's allotment (Rom 8:14-17)
Designated for place of a son (Eph 1:4-5)
Seated in celestials; to display grace in oncoming eons (Eph 2:6)
Will judge the world & messengers (1 Cor 6:1-3)
His body; complement of One completing all in all (Eph 1:23)
To display riches of His grace (Eph 2:7)

ELOHIM/GODS = MEN
Moses appointed elohim to Pharoah (Ex 7:1)
Judges (Ex 21:6; 22:8,9)
El judges the elohim (Psalm 82:1)
In the law ... I say you are gods (John 10:34, from Psalm 82:6)
Many gods and lords, but for us there is one God, the Father (1 Cor 8:5-6)
The god of this eon blinds ... (2 Cor 4:4)
Whose god is their bowels ... (Phil 3:19)
There are those "termed a god" (2 Thes 2:4)

EONS
In accord with the purpose of the eons (Eph 3:11)
Before times eonian (2 Tim 1:9-10; Titus 1:1-3; 1 Cor 2:6-8)
Present wicked eon (Gal 1:3-5)
The current eon (1 Tim 6:17)
The eon of this world (Eph 2:2)
Not only this eon, but also the impending (Eph 1:21)
Impending eon (Mt 12:32; Mk 10:30; Lk 18:30; Heb 6:5; Eph 1:21)
Oncoming eons (Eph 2:7)

All the eons (Jude 1:25)
End of the eon (Matt 13:39; 13:49; 24:3; 28:20)
End of the eons (Heb 9:26; 1 Cor 10:11)
He will reign forever (Luke 1:33) "for the eons"
They shall reign forever & ever (Rev 22:5) "for the eons of the eons"
He must be reigning **until** (1 Cor 15:25)
The god of this eon (2 Cor 4:4)

EXPECTATION
Celestials (Eph 1:3; 2:6; Phil 3:20), In Christ snatched away (1 Thes 4:13ff)
Israel (Matt 5:5), Wicked taken away (Matt 24:37ff)

HAPPY GOD
Good news of the happy God (1 Tim 1:11)

LAKE OF FIRE
Beast & false prophet (Rev 19:20)
Devil (20:10)
Second death (20:13-15)
In new heavens & earth (21:7-8)

LEGALISM
Beware ... human tradition – elements of world (Col 2:8-23)
Turning back to infirm & poor elements ... scrutinizing days (Gal 4:8)
Christ frees us ... yoke of slavery (Gal 5:1)
Deciding for one day over another (Rom 14:5)

PAUL'S EVANGEL
Came thru a revelation (Gal 1:11)
To **complete** the word of God (Col 1:25)
My evangel (Rom 2:16; 16:25-26)
Evangel of Uncircumcision/Circumcision (Gal 2:7)
As the rest of scriptures (2 Pet 3:15-16)
Message recvd as word of God (1 Thes 2:13)
Callousness ... until complement of nations (Rom 11:25)
Forfeits right to be supported (1 Cor 9:12)
Ambassadors (2 Cor 5:20)
Paul abandoned (2 Tim 1:15; 4:16; Acts 21:20)

RESURRECTION
Resurrection anticipated by Jews (Job 19:25-27; Hos 13:14; John 11:24)
Some say resurrection already occurred (2 Tim 2:18)

RIGHTLY DIVIDING
Correctly cutting the word of truth (2 Tim 2:15)
All Scripture inspired (2 Tim 3:16)
Pattern of sound words (2 Tim 1:13)
Try the things that differ (Phil 1:10 KJV)

SECRET ("musterion")
Secret wisdom concealed (1 Cor 2:7)
Administrators of God's secrets (1 Cor 4:1)
Not all sleep, but all changed (1 Cor 15:51)
Making known secret of His will – head up all in Christ (Eph 1:10)
To make known the secret of the evangel (Eph 6:19)
Not known in past; now being revealed (Eph 3:3ff)
Members of His Body (Eph 5:32)
To complete word of God—the secret concealed... (Col 1:26)

SPECULATION
Learn not to be disposed above what is written (1 Cor 4:6)

TRINITY
Grace & truth thru Christ; God no one has seen (John 1:18)
One God the Father, and one Lord Jesus Christ (1 Cor 8:6-7)
The Son seated at God's right hand (Heb 1:3)

Index

This overview contains the thoughts and opinions of the author, and is a work in progress as his study of the Scriptures continues. Some things that God has revealed are very clear. That Christ died for our sins; that He was entombed; and that He was roused (1 Corinthians 15:3) is clear. That all are to be ultimately reconciled to God thru the work of Christ is also very clear (1 Corinthians 15:20-28). But on many specifics in the Scriptures there are a variety of interpretations and opinions, and none should conclude they have the complete and final understanding on these matters that are less clear. The reader is encouraged to consider various opinions, but to study and to think for himself. Within the Body of Christ we should study and discuss our understandings so as to mutually reach a more complete understanding of that which God has revealed.

Unless otherwise noted, Scriptures are taken from the Concordant Literal New Testament and the Concordant Version of the Old Testament. Concordant Publishing Concern, 15570 West Knochaven Road, Santa Clarita, CA 91387 (www.Concordant.org)

Grace Evangel Fellowship:
P O Box 6, Wilmore, KY 40390
www.GraceEvangel.org

About the Author

Bob Evely is Vice President with a national company, overseeing sales, sales training, servicing, marketing, and special projects. He is a graduate of Oakland University (Rochester, Michigan) and has a Master of Divinity (M.Div.) Degree from Asbury Theological Seminary (Wilmore, Kentucky). For three and a half years Bob served as pastor of the Canton and West Point United Methodist Churches in Salem, Indiana; and for five years he served as pastor of the Open Door Free Methodist Church in Nicholasville, Kentucky. Both were bi-vocational positions, with Bob supporting his family through full time employment.

In May 2002 Bob resigned as pastor of Open Door Free Methodist Church to found Grace Evangel Fellowship, an independent ministry/church based in Wilmore, Kentucky. His ministry includes writing, speaking, teaching, and corresponding via email.

Bob resides in Wilmore, Kentucky with his wife Jill (since 1975). Originally from the Romeo, Michigan area the Evelys have five children: Cris (Jen), Dusty (Sharon), Chad (Molly), Kari (Jason), and Scott (Martha). As of this writing they are blessed with 7 grandchildren (Elinor, Allison, Abby, Lilli, Livi, Annabelle, and Alex).

Jill homeschooled all five children, and for 20 years represented Sonlight Curriculum as a consultant. Besides staying busy as a wife, mother, and grandma, Jill is an accomplished soap maker (PrairieKari.com) and she continues to encourage parents interested in homeschooling their children.

The author can be contacted at Grace Evangel Fellowship, P O Box 6, Wilmore, Kentucky 40390; or via email bob@GraceEvangel.org

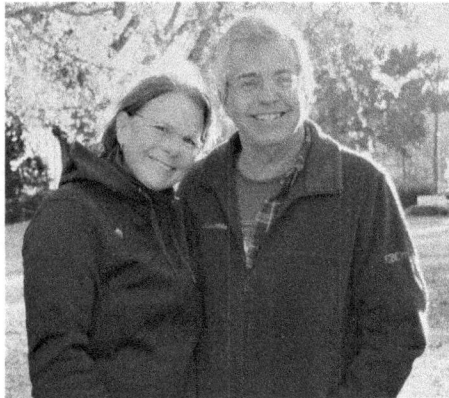

Books by Bob Evely

At the End of the Ages; the Abolition of Hell (2002)

The Visitation; An Overview of the New Testament, Part One (2018)

The Waiting; An Overview of the New Testament, Part Two (2018)

The Pause; An Overview of the New Testament, Part Three (2018)

The Return of the King; An Overview of the New Testament, Part Four (2018)

Many shorter writings can be found at GraceEvangel.org

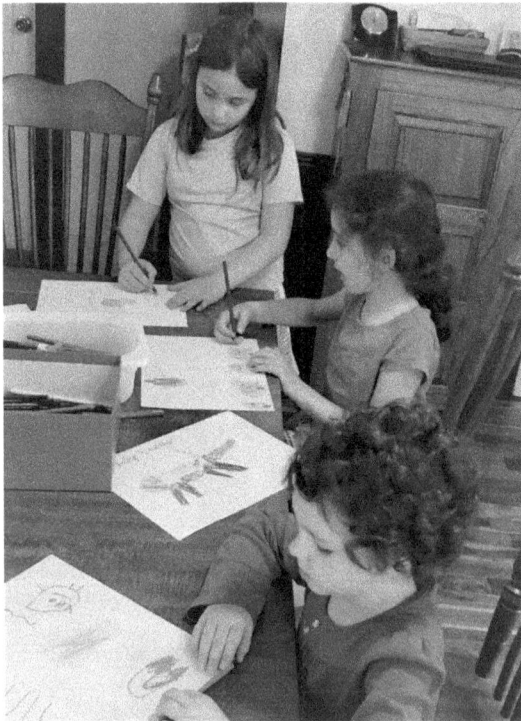

Book Artists at Work
Allison, Elinor & Lilli Evely

www.ingramcontent.com/pod-product-compliance
Lightning Source LLC
LaVergne TN
LVHW011353080426
835511LV00005B/263